Fulkumari

Pinaki Bhattacharya

Edited and introduced by David Selim Sayers

PICT Books

Paris Institute for Critical Thinking

PICT Books

All rights reserved. No part of this book may be reproduced, stored in a retrieval system, or transmitted by any means, electronic, mechanical, photocopying, recording, or otherwise, without prior permission of the publisher.

Copyright © Pinaki Bhattacharya, 2025
Introduction copyright © David Selim Sayers, 2025

PICT logo by Sage Waters

Published by the Paris Institute for Critical Thinking (PICT)

www.parisinstitute.org

ISBN: 978-2-494635-13-5

Dans Paris il y a une rue ;
dans cette rue il y a une maison ;
dans cette maison il y a un escalier ;
dans cet escalier il y a une chambre ;
dans cette chambre il y a une table ;
sur cette table il y a un tapis ;
sur ce tapis il y a une cage ;
dans cette cage il y a un nid ;
dans ce nid il y a un œuf ;
dans cet œuf il y a un oiseau.

L'oiseau renversa l'œuf ;
l'œuf renversa le nid ;
le nid renversa la cage ;
la cage renversa le tapis ;
le tapis renversa la table ;
la table renversa la chambre ;
la chambre renversa l'escalier ;
l'escalier renversa la maison ;
la maison renversa la rue ;
la rue renversa la ville de Paris.

— Paul Eluard

Contents

Fulkumari: A PICT Story	i
Preface	vii
Prologue	1
Introductions	3
Rue Stephenson	5
Arjun and Akram	7
The Holy Grail of Vegetables	10
Kinnar-Mithun	12
Rajshahi Medical College	15
Babla Bhai	17
Charu Mama	20
The Dissection Room	24
The Closed Gate	26
Growing a Beard	30
The Patient	32
Dr. Tara	34
Interlude	37
Panch Phoron	39
Behula's Raft	41
The Life of a Bird	43
Civil War	47
Boro Jethu's Mole	49
A Bowl of Milk	52
Nirman Haji's Place	56
The Leader Who Failed Maths	59
Dadhichi's Bones	61
Baba's Final Journey	64

Growing Pains	69
Ramu	*71*
The Sliced Egg	*74*
Liquid Symphony	*77*
Thunder and the Coconut Tree	*81*
Karna	*83*
Interlude	87
The Divine in the Details	*89*
Dreaming, We Become Human	*92*
The Hospital	95
The Missed Farewell	*97*
Indra's Blessing	*99*
Music Is Life	*102*
The Second Heart Unbent	*104*
Melody of Trees	*106*
After Fulkumari	109
Kojagari Night	*111*
Jesus of Palestine	*114*
Humiliating Scrutiny	*117*
Flames Engulf the Landscape	*120*
A Nation of Refugees	*125*
Bhusuku Is a Bengali	*129*
The Return	133
A Bird with Clipped Legs	*135*
The Final Return	*137*
Eternal Recurrence	*139*
Epilogue	141

Fulkumari: A PICT Story

Pinaki first came to us before Covid. In late 2019, he enrolled in "Forgiveness: To Clarify the Concept," a course to be taught at the Paris Institute for Critical Thinking (PICT) by Viktoras Bachmetjevas, a philosopher colleague and friend of PICT founder Evrim Emir-Sayers. But then, before the course could begin, came Covid, and while most schools and universities engaged in a race to embrace the disgrace of "online education," no matter the cost to the well-being of their students and faculties, let alone to the theory and practice of education itself, PICT opted to stop its course program altogether until in-person classes could resume.

And so, for about two years, Pinaki remained just a name on our screens—but remain he did. He didn't withdraw his enrollment, and neither did he get restless about when the course would finally start. We had no idea who he was or how he was passing the pandemic, and we were also somewhat torn about whether he was monumentally patient or had simply forgotten about us, but either way, as PICT focused on open-access podcasts and publications to bridge the gap imposed by Covid, his name on that enrollment list was one of those crucial details that reassured us there was, indeed, an other shore to reach.

Finally, lockdown restrictions were lifted, PICT restarted its in-person program, and Viktoras came to Paris to teach. And there, on the first day, as if he'd only just enrolled, was Pinaki. We learned that he came from Bangladesh, that he was a political refugee, and that he viewed the seminar as part of his personal quest to come to grips with his persecution. Soon enough, the course was over, but Pinaki's involvement with PICT had only just begun. He took many other PICT courses, even though on certain occasions, he seemed somewhat more absorbed by his mobile phone (at that point, we had no idea about the intensity of his online activism).

Fulkumari

During one of those courses, I found out how Pinaki had passed the pandemic. It was a one-day workshop called "Writing Is Rewriting," for which I challenged writers to bring in material they'd already been working on. Pinaki came in with a collection of vignettes he'd written during lockdown, loosely structured around some interactions he'd had with a rat in his apartment while alone and isolated in pandemic Paris. The collection ranged from childhood to recent memories, political to philosophical musings, and historical to mythological excursions, all brought together by Pinaki's distinct tone and voice, his personal and cultural outlook, and, of course, the rat herself—that is, Fulkumari.

As intrigued as I was, that was all I heard from Fulkumari for a long time. Then came that fateful, slightly overcast day when Evrim and I met up with PICT co-founder Maria Matalaev on the outskirts of Paris and later decided to walk back home along the Seine in order to see some neighborhoods we'd normally have little occasion to visit. I remember a soft drizzle starting up, and then, amidst the first drops of rain, a familiar figure appearing in the distance—it was Pinaki! Turns out we were quite close to his office, and he was out for a break. He invited us over for coffee, and our conversation rekindled my curiosity about that rat. Once back home, I wrote to him, stating my confidence in the manuscript and my wish to work with him one-on-one to bring out its full potential. And thus began my deep dive into the world of Fulkumari.

Pinaki and I started spending at least one morning a week revising the manuscript. It was a challenge of firsts for both of us: Pinaki had already written close to twenty books in Bengali, but except for a human rights report, this was his first work in English, and it was the closest by far he'd ever come to writing narrative fiction. I, for my part, had never worked with an author who wrote in such a discernible voice on things that I knew so little about. I had to consider elements of content, such as the accessibility of cultural and historical references to lay anglophones such as myself, and, at least as importantly, elements of style, which meant providing the tools for Pinaki to shape the English language into the most effective vehicle for his own unmistakable form of expression.

I was excited to see how well these concerns tied in with other, ongoing projects, particularly ones I was conducting with Evrim Emir-Sayers. Firstly, Pinaki's work didn't just open my eyes to the global significance of Bengali history, the hardships and achievements by which it has been marked, and the culture and values that have carried its people to this day. It also offered me an anticolonial discourse, related to what Graeber and Wengrow called the "Indigenous Critique," that proceeds with a full, in-depth awareness of so-called Western civilization while at the same time not losing the distance and perspective required to subvert it in ways that may seem taboo to insiders. How often, for instance, do we hear Europeans argue that twentieth-century colonialism may well have persisted to this day if not for the intervention of fascism? And how often do we hear them toy with the idea that Jesus was a Palestinian?

While I'd attempted to reconstruct such an anticolonial discourse from Ottoman literary sources in my own recent *Gender in Ottoman Constantinople*, here it was being deployed, in the first person, by Pinaki himself—and in the language of the colonizer to boot! This second aspect tied in especially well with the scholarly introduction that Evrim and I wrote for Gün Benderli's *A Cuisine of Exile*, in which we argued that English is up for grabs, that as the lingua franca of our day, it can no longer be monopolized and weaponized by a "native speaking" minority of users, and that, rather than being a language that's translated from, it must become a language that's translated into, adapting itself to new ways of thinking and speaking as well as new things to think and speak about, thereby untethering itself from its provincial origins and coming into its own as a true lingua franca.

But as Pinaki and I were ensconced in our little cocoon, busily chipping away at the manuscript, the outside world didn't come to a halt, and two events occurred that would significantly affect the fortunes of the book. The first was the decision by the Paris Institute for Critical Thinking to launch its own non-profit publishing house, PICT Books. It soon emerged that most of our initial titles shared themes of exile, dispossession, appropriation, and cultural exchange, including not only the two books above but also others such as Evrim Emir-Sayers' *The Veil of Depiction: Painting in Sufism and Phenomenology*, Zachary J. Foster's *The Invention of Palestine*, and Gaye Petek's *History of Turks in France*. I felt that Pinaki's book fit right in—or should I say that I was loath to even think about it fitting in anywhere else? Thankfully, everyone agreed, and so, *Fulkumari* found its home at PICT Books.

The second event was somewhat more epochal. In the summer of 2024, as Pinaki and I were nearing the end of our work, there was a revolution—a literal revolution—in Bangladesh. It overthrew a regime with deep historical connections to many issues Pinaki raises in this book, the very same regime that had driven Pinaki himself into exile. At first, it seemed like just another case of street protests brutally suppressed by a state—another one of those cautionary tales about the futility of militant, grassroots political activism that are peddled to us so globally and incessantly by the mass media that their conclusion seems foregone. But then, the people of Bangladesh offered us all a heady reminder that there are no foregone conclusions, that physical forces cannot be dammed by discourse alone, and that everything can change in the blink of an eye: the regime fell, the government fled, and the revolutionaries took over.

Fulkumari: A PICT Story

I was reminded of the 2013 Gezi Park protests in Istanbul, which Evrim and I had the enormous privilege of witnessing firsthand, and which she poignantly described as the "possibility of an impossibility." As Evrim taught me back then, and as Pinaki reminds us now, a revolutionary moment is not to be measured solely by its material achievements, but even more importantly by the new vistas it opens up before our eyes and the new paths it opens up beneath our feet. In the case of both Turkey and Bangladesh, I was moved to see that the "new" in question is very much also an "old": an ideal of multicultural, multireligious, multilinguistic coexistence that was the measure of tranquility and peace for centuries before being rudely (and, one can only hope, briefly) shoved aside by the divisive forces of ethnoreligious nationalism.

For the first time since Gezi Park, I also found myself in a completely unexpected front-row seat to the ongoing political turmoil. Pinaki started taking urgent phone calls during our editing sessions to consult a wide range of people in Bangladesh regarding last-minute developments, and I started to truly grasp what a valuable and influential voice he was for those carrying out the revolution on the ground. And as I saw a new chapter in the history of Bangladesh being written before my eyes, I sensed how some of the more sorrowful stories Pinaki had told in his book began to acquire a new, hopeful hue.

Even now, as we put the final touches on *Fulkumari* as you will come to know it, I'm happy to share that the PICT story accompanying the book is far from over. Quite some time ago, Pinaki had already floated the idea of launching an initiative similar to PICT in Bangladesh, but with the political situation being what it was, it seemed like a distant dream. Then came the revolution, and shortly afterwards, Pinaki was conferring with various PICT co-founders including Evrim and Sage Waters, assembling a local team—and then, before we knew it, we received an email confirming the official registration of the Dhaka Institute for Critical Thinking in Bangladesh! Only time will tell whether the Dhaka Institute will blossom as beautifully as the Krishnachura tree that shades the canteen of Rajshahi Medical College, but we'll be sure to do our part to water its roots.

David Selim Sayers
Paris, December 21, 2024

Preface

This novel was conceived during the Covid-19 pandemic, when Bangladesh was ruled by a fascist regime. In August 2024, just before the book went to print, the regime was overthrown by a popular revolution. The revolution has brought with it a mixture of hope and uncertainty. While the former regime's supporters are still fighting for its restoration, the revolutionaries themselves are at odds over their new government. Many of the bureaucrats and generals in power are still the same, and an obsolete constitution still overshadows the people's will.

Today's Bangladesh is both the same and not the same as the one of this novel. A revolution is supposed to change everything and offer a fresh start, while in reality, it only opens the view onto an ideal that can never be fully reached. But this is precisely the value of an ideal: it gives us a standard to which we may aspire. Once we reach what we thought was the ideal, it ceases to be ideal; we then set the bar even higher and strive towards that. And so, as I witness our revolution take its course, I keenly await the new ideals it will set out for us to reach.

Pinaki Bhattacharya
Paris, October 2024

Prologue

Chandaa o Chandaa, Chandaa o Chandaa, kisane churaai teri meri nindiyaa, jaage saari rainaa, tere mere nainaa. Chanda oh Chanda, who has stolen your sleep and mine—all night long, our eyes are wide awake. The sweet memories will never let me sleep. In our Dhaka home, I used to turn up the volume on those old Hindi songs, much to the annoyance of my wife. She was never convinced that the music could only evoke my treasured memories if I played it as loudly as those powerful speakers of my childhood.

In my memory, there are three distinct threads, each shimmering with pure joy and happiness, each lasting no more than a few precious minutes. One afternoon, as a child, I stood with Ma in front of the Altafunnesa playground next to our home in Bogra. The afternoon light was so beautiful that it turned everything into gold, and the moment became the benchmark against which I measure all happy times.

The second moment was also in the afternoon, during Durga Puja. My grandfather was taking me down to the temple, just a few minutes' walk from our home. The popular Hindi song blared so loudly from the temple's speakers that I couldn't hear anything else; I could only see my grandfather towering above me and feel his index finger which I gripped with my small hand. He was of no more than average height, really, but to my childhood self he seemed a giant, and I had to reach up high to hold his hand.

In Hindu mythology, there's a realm, a celestial bridge between heaven and earth, known as the Father's Place. It's here that fourteen generations of our ancestors reside, waiting to welcome us. Upon our arrival, the eldest among them bids us farewell, embarking on his final journey to the heavenly abode. I imagine myself in the Father's Place, once again walking alongside my grandfather, my hand clutching his finger with a grip so firm it could never slip. As we traverse the landscape, a loud, melodious tune fills the air, its echoes ringing around us: *Chandaa o Chandaa, Chandaa o Chandaa, kisane churaai teri meri nindiyaa, jaage saari rainaa, tere mere nainaa.*

"I'm putting on that song again, Fulkumari," I say into the emptiness of my room, "I hope you don't mind the volume!" Like Chanda, I don't want to sleep; I want to walk the long roads just like the child I used to be, holding on to my grandfather's index finger.

Introductions

Rue Stephenson

It's the first day of lockdown in Paris. After stocking up on food, I'm dragging myself back to my apartment on Rue Stephenson. The sun dips below the horizon, setting the sky ablaze like a piece of red-hot copper. Not a single soul is to be seen anywhere about. As the light of the dying sun dances over the unadorned building, it seems to me that the structure has been waiting here for aeons just to bask in this evening's aura.

Beside the building, by the horse chestnut tree, a young lady is waiting for Bus 302 from Gare du Nord. In the light of the setting sun, her elongated shadow spills over the sidewalk and down the exasperating road. With her forlorn eyes downcast, the woman is probably thinking about the future. Suddenly, she turns restless. Her eyes light up like those of a huntress; she has caught sight of the bus. Had it been a young man instead of a bus coming down the concrete road, her penetrating gaze surely would have shattered his heart.

Who knows how many strangers have stood like this by the horse chestnut tree through all the ages past? How many hearts have leapt into the sky like iridescent comets, vanishing beyond the dark veil of clouds?

Today, it's as if I'm taking note of the bulky building entrance, with its iron and wooden ornaments, for the very first time. As I strain to push it open, its creaking greets me like a stranger.

I step into my ground floor apartment and open the window, looking out at the quiescent sidewalk and the vast, empty road. A gust of air hits my face; I can hear the Parisian winds wailing. Standing at my window, I try to grasp the meaning of these peculiar cries. The breeze seems to be carrying an invisible menace, out to devour the city on its last spring evening. No sound escapes my lips; incalculable storms are sputtering furiously in the distance.

The moon has ascended, and it strikes me that the world is just as beautiful and wistful as this silver view. But even the full moon is not without its speckles. From some shadowy corner of the world, a deadly virus has arisen and is now threatening to rob humankind of all its joy, hope, and pride. The civilisation that turned a blind eye to nature's slowly simmering rage has fallen on its face.

Is my newfound concern for the world merely a lie? All this time, I've only been worried about myself, my family, whom I yearn to see, and the people of my country, who live under fascist rule. I've been on the run for the last two years, even hiding underground for five months like a frightened rat. I've fled from one country to the next, finally finding refuge here in Paris. Now I watch on, helplessly, as the pandemic turns the world upside down.

My self-indulgent thoughts make me chuckle. Turning on the light, I pour myself a glass of red wine and sit down at the table. Ignoring the anxiety that looms over my head, I pick up my mandolin. Just as I start to play a tune I learned as a young boy, my phone starts buzzing. It's my son. It must be his bedtime, and he doesn't go to sleep without seeing his father's face on video call. For the last two years, this is the only way I've been allowed to communicate with him.

"Baba, are you being careful?"

"How much more careful can I be? I left you behind just to escape, and now I'm caged inside my apartment. It's as if my only goal in life is to survive."

"Don't you think it's important to survive?"

"It's important. But it isn't enough."

Arjun and Akram

When I left my country, I thought that running away would save me. All I could think of was survival. But then, once I began to taste the banality of exile, I started to understand the difference between living and merely existing. It's a ruthless ordeal to be entangled in the snares of mere existence—an ordeal foreign to those untouched by its cold grasp.

My life in Bangladesh was upended the day I received a call from Military Intelligence. They ordered me to come to their head office by that evening. They gave no reason, of course, but it wasn't hard to guess: I was involved in human rights, and I offered a critical perspective on my blog and social media. As someone from a Hindu and communist background, I was a particular thorn in the regime's side—people like me were supposed to be its loudest supporters, propping it up against a largely fictitious, self-fabricated threat of militant Islam.

I'd been documenting cases of enforced disappearance for a while, and so, when I got the phone call, it immediately made me think of Akram, a former youth leader of the ruling party.

One spring day, Akram received a call, just like mine, from the Major of Military Intelligence. Nobody knows why he was summoned, but he was executed the same day, without trial, as had happened to several thousand others just like him. Moments before he died, during the grim walk to his fate, he shared a fleeting conversation with his daughter on the phone. Perhaps, in those final moments, he felt the shadow of death looming over him. His voice broke into sobs, prompting his daughter to ask, "Abbu, why are you crying?"

Akram's phone stayed connected, forcing his daughter and wife to witness what came next. Down the line echoed the ominous clicks of a rifle being loaded, a prelude to the blast that was to follow. Akram, handcuffed, was shot point-blank in the chest. His wife and daughter screamed when they heard the blood-curdling bellow of the man they loved. But what was the use? It was all over.

Nonchalantly, the Major told his subordinates to remove Akram's handcuffs and scatter some bullet casings around his body. The newspapers would soon spin a tale of accidental death, a lie as transparent as it was cold. They would claim Akram was caught in the crossfire during a shootout started by his own faction. The police would say they'd retrieved two pistols and two rounds of ammunition from the scene.

Stringing word to word, they spin a web of lies. But isn't it said that *in the beginning was the Word, and the Word was with God, and the Word was God*? That *all things were made by him; and without him was not any thing made that was made*? So how did the words in our sentences come to speak lies? Why did God allow lies to plague the words that we speak? Or are we the ones to blame because we took possession of the Word and banished God far away?

In the *Mahabharata*, as the battle of Kurukshetra draws close, Arjun, poised on the brink of war, is struck by a profound dilemma. Surveying the battlefield, his eyes meet those of comrades and kin arrayed against him. The weight of impending fratricide proves too heavy to bear, and he finds himself unable to raise his weapon against his own blood. It is then that Sri Krishna, the divine incarnate, who has assumed the role of Arjun's charioteer, steps forward.

"O Arjun," says Sri Krishna, pointing at Arjun's countrymen, "delay no further and shoot your arrow."

Arjun hides his trembling hands under his clothes. "How can I do that, my friend?" he asks. "If I shoot, my kin will die."

A smile blooms on Sri Krishna's blue countenance. "What makes you think that you have the power to take someone's life?" he asks. "There is no such thing as a living creature in this world. Life is merely an illusion. You imagine that all of them have life. But they call me Jagadishwar, the God of the World. I—

with billions of stomachs, billions of mouths, billions of rays of the sun emanating from my eyes—I've wished there to be no such thing as a living being left in the world. I've wished to see a world of the dead. Therefore, I've killed them all. You think that you're going to kill them, Arjun? No, you'll merely be pretending to kill them, because they're already dead. So hurry now, Arjun. Release your arrow."

And there it is: Arjun fires his rifle. Rivulets of red trickle down Akram's chest, onto the verdant grass and the warm, black soil. Akram cries out. Before pouncing on him, the hungry vultures hesitate for an instant. They can see the blood flowing into the river. They've never seen such a river of simmering blood before. Just at that moment, the sky cracks open, and the wail of a girl is heard: "Abbu, why are you crying?"

Just like Akram, I don't understand. What is my crime? Why must I be subjected to this? But I don't want to be turned into the false statement of a press note. And I refuse to accept that I'm already dead.

I run away.

The day before I received the call, I was with my parents and younger brother. My mother had sewn a button onto my shirt. For some reason, she'd felt like cooking *kumro fuler bora* for me, a Bengali delicacy made with pumpkin flowers and usually only prepared on special days. Here, in the unfamiliar Parisian soil, there are no pumpkin flowers to be found. My roots are still embedded in the soil of Bogra. They drink its waters, but its nourishment doesn't reach me anymore. They say that refugees flee to save their lives, but what is a life cut off from its roots?

The Holy Grail of Vegetables

There is a Bangladeshi shop near my apartment where I can get basic necessities such as mung beans, hilsa fish, and banana flowers. The shop is closed now, of course, but I can still order online. They take cash at the door, which suits me fine since I'm uncomfortable with entering my credit card information on a website—something I've never done in Bangladesh. Whether I like it or not, though, the pandemic is accelerating our digital exchanges. We're forced to shop online, viewing products as mere images, unable to touch or feel them before they arrive at our homes. But the products themselves aren't the only things we can't touch over the internet—the same goes for our history and culture.

Whenever I went to the Bogra market as a child, I was welcomed warmly by the vendors who knew my family. There was one elderly grocer in particular who delighted in telling me tales, painting vivid pictures of the city as it was half a century ago, an age with less people on the streets, more produce at the stands, and lives woven with simplicity and joy. He would share the names of vegetables that were commonplace back then but had since faded into obscurity.

My favourite story of his was about my grandfather, and how he used to buy squash every day. I'd never seen this so-called squash in my life, so I asked the vendor about it, and somewhat to his own surprise, he realised that the vegetable had been absent from the markets for quite some time. As he tried to describe it to me, my child's mind blew it up into the most special plant of all, a kind of holy grail of vegetables, round and golden like an orange, but with green spots to set it apart. It was only upon coming to Paris and seeing zucchini for the first time that I realised this was the squash my grandfather had loved so much. And as the vegetable made its way into my own dishes, a simple story told by an old vendor to an impressionable child grew into a link of flavour between my grandfather and myself.

The desire to communicate, to exchange, whether through goods, services, words, or dishes, is universal. For Marx, the concept of exchange went far beyond economic transactions, extending to all forms of interchange, from the market to the creation of life itself. And that's why the inherent need to exchange, when stifled, becomes the harshest of all punishments, with prisons as the most visible manifestation of its terror.

Our history is filled with tales of social ostracism, where exclusion from the community is considered a fate even worse than imprisonment. Socrates, who championed the examined life, suggesting that to truly value freedom and comfort, we must experience their absence, chose death over exile when his community put him on trial for not adhering to its customs. My own life, from the time I spent in custody to my months underground and all the way to the confinement of the pandemic, has been an object lesson in the precarity and preciousness of freedom. But to the misfit, the isolated, the exile, however free to roam, the entire world can be a prison.

Kinnar-Mithun

In twenty-first century Paris, the untimely ringing of clocks has stopped. In the hushed dawn of my room, where even silence speaks in whispers, I awaken to a symphony of chirps. It seems as though the birds have ventured right into my sanctuary. But no, it's not the winged creatures of the sky—it's two rats, small and unassuming, messengers of a realm unseen. They perch by the kitchen counter, their play halted by the crinkle of a newspaper, their eyes gleaming with an unearthly intelligence.

They seem just like the rats in Bangladesh, so much so that for a moment, I'm transported back home. And as I look more intently, the difference vanishes altogether. In their chirps, I hear the echo of Kinnar-Mithun—legendary beings, their presence a bridge between reality and imagination. In the tapestry of ancient tales, woven in the threads of the *Mahabharata*, there lived a sage's daughter, Lapita, whose kindness quenched the thirst of Kinnar-Mithun. In gratitude, they posed a question: "What do you wish for?"

Now, as I behold these two rats, mirrors of those ancient beings, a thought unfolds in the quiet of my room. If I were to offer them water, would they, too, extend the offer of a wish? My voice, a mere whisper, would break the stillness: "What can you give me?"

Their reply, a rustle in the silence, as if the breeze itself carried their words: "Become like us. We have nothing else to offer you."

Curiosity urges me onwards: "Who are you?"

Their response, a murmur like leaves in a gentle wind: "We are eternal lovers. We're never apart from each other. We bear no children. We're devoted to one another until the end of time. There is no third soul between us. Do you want this life?" This is what they asked Lapita.

"That's all?" she exclaimed.

Introductions

Do I yearn for such an existence? A life eternal, intertwined, with no lineage to call my own? Far from the roots that anchor me to my land, wandering the earth in a love only shared by another soul? The thought lingers in the air, as tangible as the morning mist.

The rats gaze upon me, their eyes void of sympathy, yet filled with a serene acceptance. They are bearers of a blissful ignorance, untouched by the tides of human emotion, existing in a world apart where memories of loves and homelands past are but fleeting shadows.

In the midst of this silent exchange, an idea catches fire. If these creatures could whisk away the burden of memory, the weight of a homeland's love and sorrow, would my heart find peace? If they could carry off with them the essence of my being, leaving behind only a shell, would the agony of longing cease?

Rajshahi Medical College

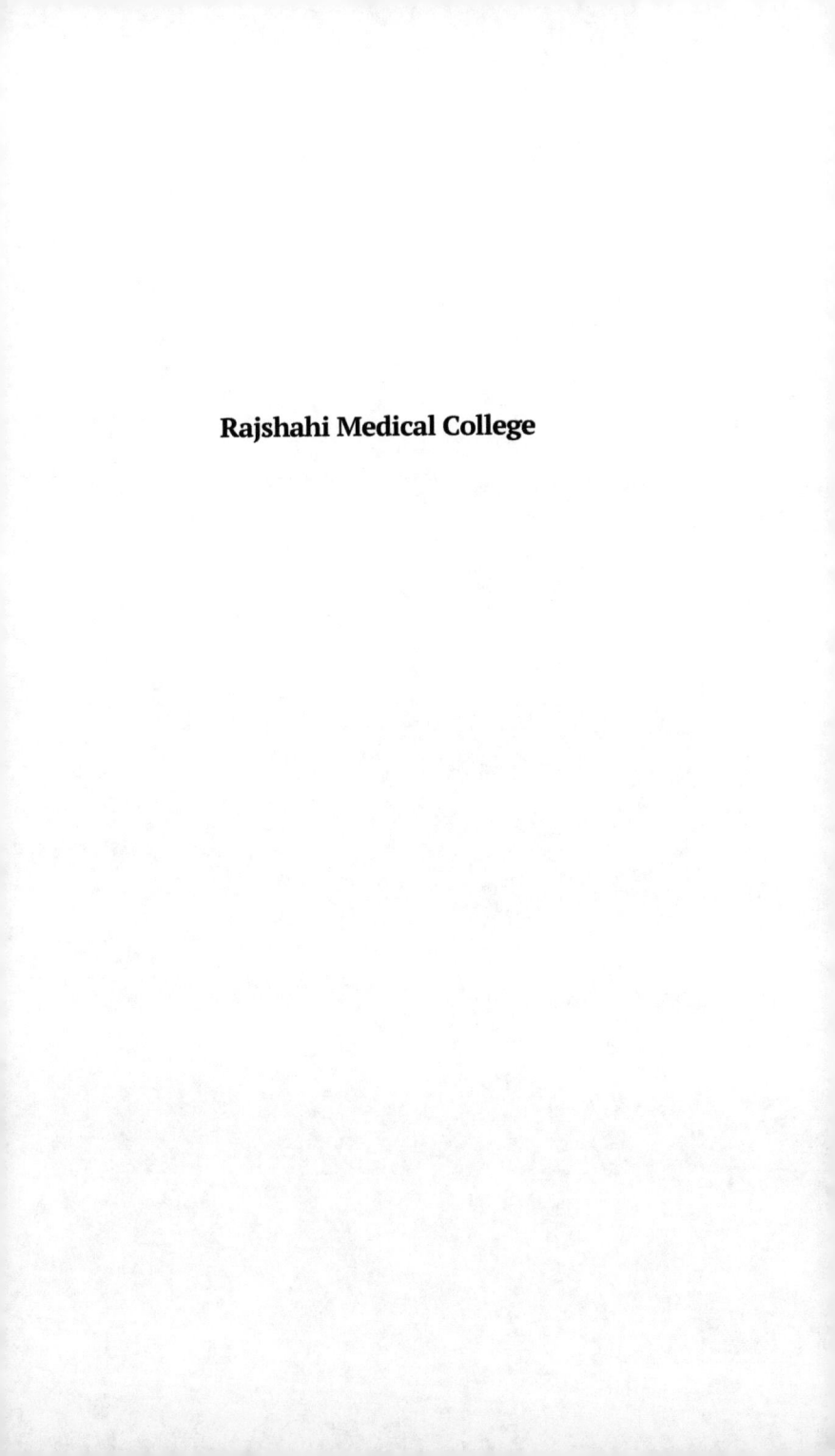

Babla Bhai

The next day, I wake up to find that dawn is gone. One of the rats is still scurrying about. When it catches sight of me, it comes to a standstill, its eyes brimming with excitement. Will it get scared if I beckon to it? Maybe I should give it a name. But what? It twitches its ears; they look like a pair of flowers balanced on top of its head. In Bengali, the flower is *ful*—but I also need a sign of affection. How about *kumar*—a young prince? Ah! I should call it Fulkumar. But it seems to be a female. Fulkumari, then. Softly, I call out to her.

"Fulkumari, where is your companion?"

No answer. Is the answer, perhaps, too terrible to be told? Did her companion somehow incur Fulkumari's disfavour? Did she forsake him because he failed to entertain her? I better be careful that the same fate doesn't befall me.

At this moment, Fulkumari seems like more than a rat to me; it's as if she's come to embody the whimsical nature of fate itself, the fate that decides who gets to survive another day in this pandemic-stricken world. She reminds me of the sultan, Shahriyar, from the *Arabian Nights*, who decreed his bride's fate based on the stories that she told. What if Fulkumari, like the sultan, is waiting to hear a story that could sway my fate? I decide to try my luck, hoping to capture her elusive attention and, perhaps, even her favour.

Just then, a beeping sound breaks the silence of the room. I turn to my phone, where a flurry of messages is flooding the screen. It's from the group of my former medical college, and all my friends are responding to one specific message. When I see it, I'm rendered speechless. The clever pilot, Captain Ali Ashraf Khan, who was always Babla Bhai to me and to all who loved him, has been claimed by the pandemic.

A rustling sound from the kitchen area tells me that Fulkumari is getting impatient. And I realise that I have my first story.

Fulkumari

"Let me tell you about Babla Bhai, Fulkumari," I begin.

Babla is what we call the Acacia tree, a symbol of enduring strength and timeless beauty. Much like that resilient tree, Babla Bhai led a deeply anchored life—anchored in youthful joy and energy. When I think of it, I can't help but contrast it with my own life, a perpetual voyage, forever in flux, never finding a place to truly call home.

His life was a tapestry of heartfelt gestures and simple joys. His favourite food was Dano milk powder. After getting his first pilot's salary, he came home with a whole tin of it and celebrated by sitting on the balcony and finishing it off all by himself, his laughter ringing through the air. But whenever he flew to Rajshahi, where his brother Babu and I attended medical college together, he saved his pilot's breakfast and gave it to Babu. One of my most treasured memories of him takes me back to Rajshahi airport. It was there that he gifted me an omelette, so perfectly cooked and buttered that I haven't tasted its like to this day.

Babu's real name is Ali Azhar Khan, and whenever Babla Bhai couldn't reach him on the phone, he'd leave him a voice message—Hello Dr. Ali Khan, this is your brother, Captain Ali Khan. As Babu played those messages to me, his chest would swell with pride.

While getting his pilot's licence, Babla Bhai used to train in a Cessna, but his daily flights over Dhaka weren't mere training sessions. They were poetic expressions of love. He'd circle over his wife's house each afternoon—they were only engaged back then—and whenever the Cessna passed by, she'd know that it was him. What a romantic! Perhaps it was she who summoned him to the other side; the virus claimed her life a few weeks ago. And how could either of them have possibly stayed without the other?

Today, it's as if I can catch sight of the Dhaka metropolis on the other side of the horizon, but all I see is the dark abyss of a cemetery, and all I hear, the sound of distant wailing. By now, the cold, white ambulance must have crossed Mohammadpur carrying Babla Bhai, shrouded in white, to be laid down in the last empty grave next to his wife. Inside the ambulance is a young man, donning the white cap worn during Muslim prayers, his eyes brimming with tears. Drawing a sharp breath, my gaze lost in the infinite void, I feel like I'm there—he's so close, but so helpless.

Charu Mama

The day meanders slowly, draped in a blanket of anxiety. My thoughts keep circling back to Fulkumari. By the time I'd shaken off my reverie, she was gone; I don't even know if she listened until the end. In an effort to distract myself, I turn to books, emails, and the churning sea of social media. But each click only unveils images of suffering and loss, a relentless stream that mirrors the outside world's affliction. Overwhelmed, I disconnect, seeking refuge in solitude.

As evening tiptoes into Paris, the city shakes off its lethargy. It's eight o'clock, and the sound of clapping and cheers reverberates through the streets—a chorus of gratitude for the tireless healthcare staff. The voices, mostly women's, carry a peculiar tone—a blend of respect and acknowledgement of the situation's gravity. Within the applause, there is an unspoken heaviness, as if the air itself were mourning the loss of yet another soul.

The clapping subsides, and life retreats back behind closed doors. In some corner of the city, intimate moments unfold: a lover tracing the contours of her beloved's face, their eyes locked in a profound exchange, a silent communion of love and fear. In my own space, I notice movement. Fulkumari is back again, her tiny form darting around, occasionally pausing to fix me with her gaze. It seems that she has accepted our unspoken pact. I prepare some crumbs and bits of cheese, an offering to entice her closer. She nibbles cautiously, her eyes flickering up to mine.

"Listen closely, Fulkumari," I say, trying to set the mood. "Let me take you back to Rajshahi Medical College, to a time of youthful dreams and aspirations, to a place where destinies intertwine under the guise of education, politics, and friendship."

The night wraps itself around us as I speak, the city's heartbeat a distant echo now. In this small, shared space, time seems to pause, allowing my story to unfurl like a bridge spanning two shores of a world turned upside down.

I stand in front of a beautiful building with my apron on. The happy faces of students, bathed in the soft morning light, brighten up the scene. Like I've just done myself, they're walking to the college from the boys' and girls' hostels, down the road that cuts through campus like the edge of a sword, with the college on one side and the hospital on the other.

The road is perhaps the best-loved spot on campus. On the college side, there are rows and rows of mango trees. The trees are probably ancient, though; I've never seen them bear fruit. There are quite a few buds, of course, but they fall off almost as soon as they appear. If you happen to step on them while walking down the road, your senses are engulfed by their intoxicating smell.

In the morning, when everyone flocks to their classes, the road is flooded with a quaint amalgamation of the students' various perfumes. No one can put a name to the scent that emerges. Strangely enough, I sometimes seem to catch the same fragrance on the streets of Paris. I've never experienced this in any other city. Is this mystifying scent of my youth emerging from the crevices of my mind, or does it come from the unseen flower of heaven?

Whenever I walk past the girls' hostel, the leaves of those barren mango trees appear particularly green to me. Even as the city of Rajshahi is gradually dried out by the Farakka Dam across the Indian border, this spot always seems to retain its peculiar shade, with a sweet, gentle breeze blowing over it.

The road never seems to end. But eventually, shattering every illusion, it does, by the Krishnachura tree standing sentinel at the entrance to the college. In its name, a fusion of the earthly and divine: Krishna, the Hindu god of love, and *chura*, crown. In February, the first month of spring, the tree erupts in a blaze of red, its blossoms a fiery testament to the renewal of life.

Fulkumari

In the blossoms of the Krishnachura tree, a poignant irony unfolds. The god of love intertwines with the legacy of martyrs, painting a canvas of passion, defiance, and loss. In 1952, under Pakistani rule, the decision to elevate Urdu to the singular state language ignited fierce resistance and a fervent struggle for the official recognition of the Bengali language. A bloody crackdown in February claimed the lives of several students, their sacrifice remembered in the blossoms of the Krishnachura tree.

The dappled light and faint shadows created by the tree merge into an illusion in a corner of the college canteen. Large and perpetually graced with neglect, its walls echo with the hum of countless stories. The food is bland and overpriced, but we don't come for the cuisine—our attraction is the canteen's operator, a man of short stature, dressed in traditional Muslim attire, his smile as constant as the northern star. His name, Charu, means "art," and we affectionately call him Charu Mama, "Uncle Art." Charu Mama is a treasure trove of tales, his words painting the history of our college in vivid strokes. No one knows the ebb and flow of its legacy better than him.

The canteen harbours a unique tradition—a slender book where we jot down our debts instead of paying right away. Each month, upon receiving our allowances, we attempt to clear our dues, but our pockets are often too shallow. With unwavering patience, Charu Mama carries these debts, allowing them to stretch out until our graduation and the onset of our internships. When we finally begin to earn a respectable salary, we joyously return to settle our old scores. And yet, Charu Mama often laments, some debts remain unpaid, lost to memory and time.

For his own part, though, Charu Mama never fulfils his contractual obligations to pay the canteen's rent or its power bills. In a silent agreement, the college administration doesn't press him for these dues. Time and time again, they're furtively covered by the senior doctors, silent benefactors acting out of deep-seated gratitude for Charu Mama's generosity during their own student years.

Amongst Charu Mama's few sorrows is his lack of a son, a void that casts a shadow over his otherwise sunny disposition. Then, one radiant morning, he announces with unmatched pride that he's now father to a boy. The canteen erupts in celebration; food flows freely, a feast marking the joyous occasion. In a moment of parental bliss, Charu Mama asks me to name his newborn. I choose Ratul, meaning "sweet," a name rooted in Hindu tradition. In an act of open-heartedness that transcends religious boundaries, he embraces the name for his son, a symbol of the unity and diversity that defines our shared existence.

The Dissection Room

Two weeks have furled their wings in the quiet embrace of isolation. I'm in the same room, standing at the same window. As I gaze upwards, the vastness of the moonlit sky seems to flow into the gaping hole in my heart. The world has been drained of its lifeblood, but the sky remains the same. It's as if the moon and the stars rise again and again in the hope that one day, the earth will return their fervent love. But over the centuries, the inhabitants of this magnificent, moonlit world have pulled out, torn apart, and shattered the hearts of so many. And to this breaking of hearts, they've given a name—civilisation.

The distant lights of other homes flicker like fickle stars, a reminder of all the quiet lives unfolding in the night. As they burn out one by one, the sky deepens into a velvety darkness, beckoning me away from the window's gaze. In a secluded corner of my room, Fulkumari awaits, still offering her companionship in the midst of a world turned inwards.

I resume my narrative, my voice feeling steady and more confident with each chapter. "Back at medical college," I begin, "every corridor and classroom was a portal to a world of discovery and dreams."

As I speak, the room around us fades away and I'm transported to the bustling campus, entering the college building via the canteen, into the main hallway with the girls' common room to my right. Its door is perpetually closed, and though our curiosity is immense, the activities that transpire within its confines remain a mystery. A little further, to the left, is the open door of the boys' common room, echoing with the vibrant chatter of budding male medics.

Farther down, behind the college principal's office, lies the dissection room. Venturing this deep into the heart of the college, one is first met with the pungent, penetrating odour of formalin. Here, rows of corpses, each a silent teacher of life's mysteries, are immersed in their preserving baths. The sensory overload is so intense it can whisk you off to a completely different reality. My initial encounter with a cadaver was an immensely profound experience. It was a moment that starkly presented me with the realities of life, death, and the intricacies of the human form. To be honest, I didn't think I'd be able to continue my studies after that first dissection. And even as I did, I often grappled with the feeling of not quite fitting in or being as adept as my peers, a private rite of passage that many of us navigate without words.

Arranging rows and rows of human limbs on the table, our teacher Khaleq Sir tells us about the falciform ligament of the liver, the coronary ligament, and the right and left triangular ligament. It's hard to make out what he says because he speaks as if he has food in his mouth. Summer, winter, or monsoon, he wears the same shirt—probably the only one he owns. It's of an earthen hue, and its collar is always drenched in sweat. Khaleq Sir is forever accompanied by the sharp odour of formalin and the sweet smell of cheap cigarettes.

Anatomy class is normally taught by graduate students, but Khaleq Sir is a senior doctor. Perhaps this means his career hasn't been very successful, but he isn't a bitter man. He always does his best to make us understand the topic, and, unlike many of his younger colleagues, he never gets angry with us, even as my mind sometimes wanders off into philosophical musings.

The body has it all—flesh, marrow, nerves, and arteries; it's just life that's missing from it. I wonder, then, if our lives are actually nothing more than the relations that we have. Patients at the last stage of life, confined to an intensive care unit, might still be breathing, their organs functioning, but because they're cut off from the rest of life, it seems like they're already dead. Is it when the connections that we once had fade into nothingness that we're truly reduced to nameless bodies? Maybe that's why it's easier to see a loved one dead than to see them in pain.

The Closed Gate

Another day slips by, bringing no new discoveries or hope but only a relentless increase in the death toll. The researchers are in frantic search of a vaccine, yet I understand all too well that such a breakthrough could take years. Do we have the resilience to withstand this wait? Viruses mutate by nature, often becoming more aggressive. Yet, on occasion, they may weaken—the only thing that seems like it could save us at this point.

The world around me appears overwhelmingly grim. The US president points the finger at China, accusing it of releasing the virus from a lab supposedly engaged in biological warfare research. Will the pandemic lead us to war? Or is it, itself, a war?

I try to arrest the downward spiral of my thoughts. It feels like they have a way of becoming real; whenever I think of someone, it isn't long before I hear they're either hospitalised or dead. I find myself avoiding thoughts of my wife and son, and I don't bring them up to Fulkumari. This silence is a pledge, a superstitious attempt to keep my loved ones safe, far from the storm of my darker thoughts.

As I think of the dying and dead, my mind drifts beyond the pandemic. In Bangladesh, a history of martyrs graces all schools, and students killed by the police or their political enemies adorn the crowns of their home institutions like so many gems. Among the student hostels at my medical college, there's one known as Pinku Hostel. Pinku was also my nickname—not that the hostel was named after me. There was a nationalist student leader called Pinku, killed on campus by his leftist rivals. Their dispute had nothing to do with socialism or nationalism, though; theirs was a battle of love. Pinku and a leftist student leader were in love with the same girl, another medical student.

The lady for whom Pinku was killed later became our teacher. She used to give us anatomy classes. She was extraordinarily beautiful, just like my mother, but she worked hard to roughen up her exquisite face. She used to say that my rebellious curls resembled a bird's nest—again, just like my mother. We never found out whose feelings she reciprocated, if any at all.

On the way from the college to the hospital, at the exact spot where Pinku's life was taken, they planted a Krishnachura tree. But unlike the one outside the canteen, the flowers on this tree were never allowed to bloom in hues of blood. Every single night, someone came and messed up its crown. It wasn't only Pinku's physical existence that had been stifled; there was someone out there who couldn't even bear the sight of his memory.

During my time on campus, another student leader was killed, this one a leftist, by an Islamist student group. His name was Jamil Akhtar Ratan. With his enchanting eyes and unruly curls, he was a hero to us. Oh, but what a cruel death it was! He was mercilessly cut down in broad daylight.

Come to think of it, I never attended a school in my homeland without a murder taking place. When I was in sixth grade at the Bogra Zilla School, it was Pallab Bhai, my senior by one grade, who was killed. With his shy gaze downcast, he used to come over to our house to be tutored by Baba. One day, a seventh grade student got into a feud with his cousin. Unable to get hold of the cousin, he decided to take Pallab Bhai's life instead. Being an only child, Pallab Bhai was very dear to his parents. After his death, his mother started behaving like a madwoman.

When I was a student at Azizul Haque College, my classmate Tapas went missing. Two days later, his decapitated body was found in a Bogra pond. He had been murdered by a couple of our college seniors; we used to see them every day. I remember them being on good terms with Tapas. To this day, I have no clue what prompted them to so brutally take his life.

The streets, halls, and buildings of colleges and universities are named after these martyrs in a display of immense pride. It's as if the certificates in the hands of Bangladeshi students are gloriously embellished with these heroes' blood. It is said that

Mother Kali demands blood in return for success—she demands a sacrifice. The students of Bangladesh give up their blood for these certificates; they sacrifice their lives.

But to many in the country, this sacrifice is in vain. There's a deep rift between students and the wider population. Rather than being seen as communal assets, colleges and universities are viewed with suspicion and reserve. The common people simply cannot embrace these institutions as their own. At the far end of the medical college campus, there's a gate that was sealed decades ago. Known as Bondho Gate—the Closed Gate—it was a casualty of feuds between the students and the slum dwellers beyond its border.

The surroundings of Dhaka University echo this sentiment, surprisingly so since the site resembles a bustling metropolis rather than a community hub. Despite the absence of local settlements around the campus, there are sporadic skirmishes between students and transport workers or Nilkhet book market vendors. I could never grasp why the students found themselves at odds with the locals, mostly families going about their daily lives with no apparent reason to cause trouble.

Ultimately, the schism is due to perceptions of education and status. Students at prestigious universities often view themselves as better than the ignorant locals, cultivating an air of superiority, alienating themselves from the broader community. On the other hand, these locals see the students, many of whom hail from other regions, as arrogant interlopers. Higher education becomes a wedge, detaching the country's youth from its roots.

Upon graduation, the students ascend to positions of influence and insist on being treated with deference. Caught in a two-hundred-year-old colonial hangover, their greatest desire is to be addressed as "Sir." Yet the common folk prefer familial titles like Bhai and Aapa—big brother and big sister—which enrage government officials. And so, nourished by a poisoned colonial well, the education system keeps churning out graduates that aren't unlike the barren mango trees lining the road of the medical college campus—full of enormous potential that never comes to fruition.

The unyielding Closed Gate serves as a pathetic symbol of exclusion, a barrier not just in physical space but entrenched in social attitudes, persisting in the collective psyche.

Growing a Beard

In some ways, confinement holds a unique appeal for a solitary refugee like me, granting me the freedom not to maintain my personal appearance. But today, in order to look less menacing for an impending doctor's appointment, I decide to shave off the beard that I've been sporting since medical college. While toiling away in front of the mirror, I notice a movement to my back; it's Fulkumari, observing the scene, startled by its novelty.

"Welcome back, little one," I say, "you know, this beard has its own tale."

The year is 1990. Like many of my peers, I'm part of the student resistance movement against the military government that has ruled Bangladesh since 1982. Not far from our hostel, behind the Closed Gate, lives a government minister under heavy guard. "Fear the tiger," the proverb goes, "and the evening begins where you stand." In my fifth year, tension between the students and the government escalates to the point where a full-scale confrontation breaks out between medical students and the minister's men right outside his residence.

I'm at a protest rally in the city centre when I'm summoned back to campus. I've been serving as secretary general of the student union for a year, and my comrades hope I can persuade the enraged students to withdraw, thereby avoiding a bloodbath. Arriving on the scene, I feel like I've stepped onto a battlefield: streets littered with stones, brickbats, debris, fires smouldering, a standoff so tense it's almost frozen.

From the other side, the police chief of Rajshahi, flanked by officers and thugs, recognises me and demands through a loudspeaker that I take the students back to campus. By that point, however, the students have been joined by local residents. For the first time, I witness the community placing its trust in the students, uniting with them in their struggle against tyranny. It's a powerful sight to behold.

Suddenly, a barrage of gunfire erupts. People flee in panic; a little boy falls to the ground right before me. I rush to help him, but he's too heavy, the blood pouring from his gunshot wound slick and unmanageable. Before I know it, the police have seized me and are beating me to a pulp. I lose consciousness, only to wake up, battered and bruised, in a police van. I'm taken to the station and accused of murdering Ziabul, the boy I tried to save. Both my knees and an arm are broken; first aid is useless, so I'm taken to the medical college hospital for treatment under police custody.

A week after I'm admitted to the hospital, my comrades smuggle me out through a bathroom window. The government has proclaimed emergency rule, and I fear what might become of me if I stay in the hands of the police. My treatment, of course, is unfinished, and one of my legs will remain shorter for the rest of my life. I'm not even able to shave myself; my comrades offer to help, but the gesture is only a painful reminder of my own impotence. That's when I decide to grow out my beard.

Another week later, the regime collapses under the weight of the protests, and a caretaker government, chosen by students, is formed. I'm able to come out of hiding and continue my studies. In three months, an election is held, ushering in the first period of civil democratic rule in my country's history. The year is 1991.

The Patient

I need more masks. People aren't even allowed to go outdoors without them anymore, let alone enter a store. The pharmacies, once abundant in supplies, are empty. Even doctors can't find any. One of them posts a video of himself on social media. "The masks are supposed to be for us doctors first, before anyone else," he says. "Why are you using them? Masks are our first line of defence, but now they're a rare commodity. How are we supposed to go on fighting without them?"

The helplessness in his voice gnaws at me, a testament to the trials endured by those I once stood alongside. Overflowing wards, people sleeping on floors, supplies running out, healthcare workers swamped: it might be a new experience for doctors in France, but it's one that I know all too well. In fact, it's the reason I'm sitting here right now, looking on as my former colleagues struggle in despair.

Back in Rajshahi, I'm doing my residency at the College Hospital. Like all residents, I'm expected to endure gruelling 16-hour shifts, a daunting task in a perpetually overwhelmed hospital that never turns away a patient and often accommodates three to four times its capacity. In an effort to mitigate the shortage of essential medicine, we young doctors contribute to a secret fund, pooling resources from our modest salaries to purchase emergency supplies. Visits by pharmaceutical representatives bearing free samples are always a happy occasion, their contributions significantly bolstering our secret stockpile.

On that particular night, alone on admission duty, I'm faced with a surge of patients, all headed for emergency services, stretching the hospital's resources thinner than ever. Around dawn, having tended to patient after patient for hours on end, I seek a brief respite in the doctors' room, but my nap is cut short by a nurse's urgent wake-up call. A woman is screaming, piercing the ward's silence, keeping the others from getting some much-needed rest. Frustrated and sleep-deprived, I confront her harshly. To my horror, her screams cease, replaced by silent tears. A shattering realisation: her pain is real, not an act like I'd encountered before. Diagnosed with brain cancer, she's enduring unimaginable suffering.

The incident broke me. I understood that my heart wasn't strong enough for this path. The guilt of my insensitive words, uttered to a soul in true agony, has weighed on me ever since. It's a burden I carry, a constant reminder of the compassion I lacked in a moment that mattered most. This pain, this regret, is mine to bear for a lifetime. I doubt I will share it even with Fulkumari.

Most pharmacies are closed, but I manage to find one that's still lit amongst the dimming streets. I approach the lady at the counter.

"Can I have some masks?" I ask, my voice nearly cracking with urgency.

"Sorry, we don't have any," she says, her tone a mixture of fatigue and regret.

"You know the shops won't let us enter without a mask. What am I supposed to eat if I can't buy anything?"

"Please, give me your phone number, and I'll inform you as soon as we get new stock. But don't expect a surgical mask." She points to the piece of cloth covering her own face. "Would something like this do?"

Her suggestion, doubtful yet pragmatic, cuts through my despair. A nod is all I can muster as I entrust myself to her words and acknowledge the sliver of hope I've been handed. A cloth mask, no longer just a piece of fabric, but a treasure in these shadowy times.

Dr. Tara

Fulkumari starts her day before me. She seems excited today; I can hear her rapid footsteps dancing on the wooden floor. I myself stayed up late last night, indulging in the laziness of an extended morning sleep. Actually, waking up has always been a struggle for me. Even back at medical school, my roommates would often rush off to class while I was still in bed. The most precious and enjoyable sleep is when you wake up for some reason and then drift off again.

As I prepare my breakfast, she watches me intently.

"What's your plan today, Fulkumari?"

She starts darting back and forth. Clearly, she just wants to play.

"Great, today'll be our game day, then! What kind of game should we play?"

Suddenly, a sweet childhood memory comes to me—a memory of magic.

"Would you like to watch some magic, Fulkumari?"

She calms down. It seems she's ready for the show, though she does look a bit apprehensive. A doubt enters my mind: should I really deceive her with my magic tricks? But Hindu mythology teaches us that the whole world is an illusion. If even God can play magic with us, what's wrong with a little magic of our own?

As a child, I'd come down with a strong fever three or four times a year. Ma would cover my pillow with a polythene sheet and I'd lie down in bed, resting my head on the cold plastic. Then, she'd take a mug of water from a bucket and pour it over my head until it trickled down along the polythene and back into the bucket. Once the water in the bucket was completely warm, she'd take it away and come back with cold water again, repeating the process.

Delirious with fever, I'd lie motionless under my blanket. Sleep would refuse to come and dark rings would form around my eyes. It was as if my only job was to blankly stare at the ceiling day and night. Baba would only bring in the doctors when the fever was too stubborn to yield to our efforts alone. My favourite was Dr. Tara. His nickname was "the star," and his handsome face was perpetually adorned with a sweet smile. I can still see that smile when I shut my eyes.

Dr. Tara was one doctor I was never scared to see. When he sat on my bed and gently stroked my head, I could swear that my fever had already vanished. Once, during a visit, he retrieved a handkerchief from his pocket, folded it into a peculiar shape, and held it up to me. "Can you guess what this is?" he asked.

I spared it one glance before shutting my eyes again. "It's a bird."

"Good. But son, this isn't really a bird. Look more closely." He wiggled his hand with a magician's practised ease.

I looked again, and this time, all I could see was a simple handkerchief. Folding it up neatly, Dr. Tara put it back in his pocket. "What I just showed you is a magic trick," he said. "They perform it at the circus. If you'd like, you can learn it too and do it even better." That's when I made up my mind to learn the few tricks I'm sharing with Fulkumari today.

The same Dr. Tara came to me as a patient when I was a resident at Rajshahi Medical College. I was on duty at the coronary care unit, and Dr. Tara was admitted after suffering a massive heart attack. His wife looked at me with her tear-stained face. "Pinku," she said, "please save your Uncle Tara somehow." Taking his pulse, I noticed his heart fluttering—ventricular extrasystole. There were twelve cardiac monitors at the ward, and each of them was occupied by a patient. I stayed up with Dr. Tara all night, feeling his pulse. Somehow, he survived.

Whenever I closed my eyes that night, I could see Dr. Tara walking past the Altafunnesa playground in front of our house, his stethoscope around his neck. It seemed like all the beauty that the world had to offer had coalesced solely around him. That incomparably magnificent man would alone become the possessor of every charm and everyone's trust. It had been this sight that made me dream of one day walking past the same playground as a doctor myself, stethoscope round my neck, illuminating the path down which I strolled.

I did end up a doctor, but the remainder of my dream remained just that—a dream. Perhaps it'll always stay that way. And perhaps that's for the best; walking down the path like that, engulfing everything around him in his light—that was something only meant for Dr. Tara. It wouldn't suit anyone else.

Interlude

Panch Phoron

The stillness of the night wraps itself around me, a cloak woven from threads of solitude and introspection. Fulkumari, my unexpected companion, has disappeared into the crevices of my modest kitchen space, leaving me to ponder the tales I've spun into the silence. My stories, it seems, haven't been enough to captivate her. Or perhaps, in her own mysterious way, she listens from afar, an unseen audience to my solitary musings.

Sometimes, my life in Bangladesh feels like a distant dream, blurred and indistinct, but it comes into sharp focus in the flavours and aromas that beckon from my kitchen. As I add *panch phoron* to my fried potatoes, I'm transported back to the bustling streets of Bogra, to the laughter and warmth of a family table long left behind. The dishes I prepare are tributes to my mother's culinary prowess, recreations of her simple yet hearty meals. Due to the constraints of poverty, vegetables took centre stage in her kitchen, and they have pride of place in mine, their vibrant colours and textures an ode to creativity and resilience.

It wasn't my mother who taught me to cook, though—it was exile. I learned it in Eragny, amidst the tranquil beauty of the Oise River, where I was first registered as a refugee upon my arrival in France. The poetic names of the places I encountered there, like Pontoise and Conflans fin d'Oise, whispered stories of a land steeped in history and charm. The river, where water met sky in a harmonious dance, became my sanctuary, a place where I could escape the relentless march of time.

Cooking allowed me to blend the spices and flavours of my heritage with the nuances of French cuisine, and the dishes I prepared became my testament to a life lived in the margins, my rebellion against the anonymity of exile, my celebration of connection through the universal language of food. And so, as I sit here in the dim light of my apartment, a plate of food before me,

I'm not just a man eating his dinner; I'm a storyteller, a keeper of traditions, a wanderer on a journey to find his place in the tapestry of humanity. Like the meals I prepare, my story is an ever-evolving feast, rich with the flavours of the past and the promise of tomorrow.

A subtle rustling alerts me to Fulkumari's return, her presence like a flicker of light in the darkness. She emerges from the shadows, her small form tiptoeing across the floor with quiet determination. It's as if she senses the unfinished tales that linger in the air, like that last whiff of *panch phoron*, waiting for a voice to bring them back to life. I welcome her with a nod as she settles into her familiar spot.

She watches with an air of bemusement as I embrace the ritual of eating with my hands, a practice that dances on the edges of peculiarity in European culture. Here, where the fork reigns supreme, the custom of dining hand to mouth is like a forgotten melody, its rhymes and rhythms unknown. "Listen, Fulkumari," I say, "in the West, they often say, 'You are what you eat.' This food—it's an extension of me. Why should I let a fork, a cold, impersonal thing, come between myself and an integral part of my being? Would you?"

Behula's Raft

More than a month has passed since the lockdown began. Tens of thousands have lost their lives in France alone. Many have failed to evade the jaws of death despite staying cooped up in their houses, hiding like frightened rats from an invisible killer who cares nothing for the technology and myriad instruments—or the foolhardy arrogance—that have taught us we're the conquerors and masters of nature.

"You seem lost in thought," Fulkumari whispers from her corner, her voice as soft as a breeze.

"I was thinking of an old tale from Bogra," I reply.

Bogra, once known by the magnificent name of Pundravardhana, was the heart of ancient Bengali civilisation. In Pundravardhana, there once lived a merchant whose ships could sail the seven seas. The splendour of his business was as magnificent as the full moon; and so, he was called Chaand Saudagar—the Moon Merchant. But Chaand Saudagar had a quarrel with Manasa, the goddess of nature. Manasa wanted him to bow down before her in worship. Her wish was not unreasonable. Human beings are the children of nature and should feel pride in paying respect to their mother. But the arrogant Chaand Saudagar refused to obey, and his refusal ignited Manasa's wrath. Infuriated, she cursed him, vowing to end his bloodline.

Soon enough, all of Chaand Saudagar's sons began to die from snake bites until only one, Lakshindar, remained. When he married, his father constructed a bridal chamber for him that no snake could penetrate. On their wedding night, Lakshindar and his wife, Behula, entered the iron chamber. The air hummed with anticipation, and the moon hid behind the clouds, as if unwilling to witness the tragedy about to unfold. Making a mockery of Chaand Saudagar's precautions, Manasa sent Kalnagini—the black cobra, deadliest of serpents—to fulfil the curse. After the marriage was consummated, Lakshindar was bitten and died. Behula, ensnared in a spell, slept soundly.

Awakening to the horrible scene, Behula took an oath to save her husband. On a flimsy raft, with Lakshindar's body by her side, she abandoned herself to the river to appease Mother Manasa. Behula spurned her father-in-law's grand ships—vessels that could slice through the waves like a celestial sword. Instead, she chose a raft woven from banana tree trunks, their leaves stitched together with threads of courage.

Behula, why forsake the marvels of technology? Why sail towards the unknown on a humble raft?

She pushed her raft into the river's embrace. The current carried her through emerald forests, where monkeys chattered their secrets. She floated beneath the sun's golden gaze, her fingers trailing in the water. The raft danced with each ripple, she felt the sun's warmth on her cheeks, tasted her own tears on her lips. She's part of this—the river, the trees, the sky. And when the storm came—a tempest that tore at the heavens—Behula clung to her banana raft. Lightning cracked the sky, rain lashed her skin, but she held fast. Behula rode the fury, her heart a compass, her husband's rotting body by her side.

When dawn finally broke, the storm retreated, leaving Behula adrift on a tranquil sea. Her raft, battered but unyielding, was carrying her off to lands unknown. She closed her eyes, listening to the waters whisper, softer now: you're saved not by what you conquer, but by what you embrace.

Today, there's a Behula next to every single one of us as we travel down the river on our isolated rafts. All the might and splendour of Chaand Saudagar—the ships that sail the seven seas—have proven to be worse than useless. Our hope lies in the love and humility of Behula; it's the only thing that can save humankind from the wrath of Mother Manasa.

The Life of a Bird

I awake to the soft light of a Parisian morning, the habitual quiet of the lockdown pierced by a crescendo of birdsong, growing more vibrant with each passing moment. I understand my dream now: I was amidst a kaleidoscope of birds, their feathers a vivid tapestry of colours, flitting around me in a symphony of delicate chirps and melodies. Each of them sang a note of enchantment, weaving a lullaby that cradled my senses in an otherworldly calm.

Peeking through my window, I behold a scene that makes me wonder if I'm still asleep: the streets and rooftops are alive with the flurry of wings and the joyous calls of birds. It seems they've come to reclaim their lost territories, deserted by human invaders, and are weaving their presence into the fabric of the vacant city. Hushed by the pandemic, the world outside is finding its way back to its original voice.

Fulkumari is here as well. Gracefully, she moves around the room, her steps seeming to echo the rhythm of the birds' melodious chorus. She's dancing along to their song, her body united with their voices in shared jubilation. Theirs is a victory over the relentless greed of human civilisation, a reclamation of nature's rightful place. Such a momentous occasion should be celebrated indeed.

"You know, Fulkumari," I say, almost apologetically, "I could count as a bird, too. It was Rashid Sir, our class teacher in seventh grade, who first called me that—a bird."

Rashid Sir was teaching us about the zoo, *chiriyakana* in Bengali—the place where *chiriya*s dwell. I raised my hand to inquire about the unfamiliar word.

"Rashid Sir, what does *chiriya* mean?"

"You don't understand? Well, I suppose that makes you a *chiriya*, too."

He meant to put me in my place, implying I wasn't human but rather an animal that belonged in a zoo. For some strange reason, the man had never been able to stand me. Once, I'd come down with a fever after my little sister Bulbuli hit me in the face with the edge of a cardboard, breaking a small bone in my nose. When I finally returned to school a few days later, Rashid Sir asked me why I'd been absent.

"I had a fever, Sir."

"Why a fever?"

It was always like that with him; he'd say things just to make me feel uncomfortable. And he didn't actually know what *chiriya* meant—it's a Hindi word, and it means bird.

There was a Bengali poet by the name of Jibanananda Das. He took his life by surrendering to a speeding tramcar, and that even though his name, Jibanananda, speaks of life and joy. One of his poems goes like this:

> I am waiting for the life of a bird,
> You are waiting for the life of a bird.
>
> Perhaps, after thousands of years have slipped by,
> Whilst gliding through the blue sky amidst the last remnants
>   of winter—
> On our way to the sea—
>
> It will dawn upon us
> That this is how we wanted to fly away
> Thousands of years ago.

There's another Bengali poem, by Al Mahmud, that I used to love as a student. At the time, I didn't care so much for any deeper meaning it held; I just used it as a glorified excuse to cut class:

> All of you are studying, learning to be human,
> Let me just be a bird and learn to be wild.

Interlude

The French word for "teacher" is also "professor." A professor is someone who can profess something—announce it and claim it to be true. Today, I must convey my gratitude to Rashid Sir; he managed to profess my life. He was right about me being a *chiriya*. That's what I am now—a bird. Deprived of a place to call home, all I do is flit about and get chased away.

I look out the window again and wonder how long the triumphant birdsong will last.

Civil War

Boro Jethu's Mole

After my doctor's visit, I decide to keep up my shaving routine, but it takes me some time to regain the skill I had as a young man. One morning, in front of the mirror, my hand twitches, and I give myself a deep cut. As I flinch from the flowing blood, so does Fulkumari, who is once again watching from behind.

"Now, that gives me a story to tell," I say, catching my breath, "it's about my uncle Chitta, as careless with his blade as I am."

Uncle Chitta—or Boro Jethu, as we called him—had a mole on his jawline, and he often cut it while shaving. Whenever he did, he'd dip a cotton swab in Dettol and press it long and hard onto the cut. And whenever he was engrossed in study or deep in concentration, he'd twist and pull at the mole. When people asked him why, he'd chuckle and say that doing so helped him think more clearly.

Baba had eleven siblings, all of whom grew up in our Bogra house. Boro Jethu was the eldest, and eighteen years Baba's senior. He studied nuclear physics with distinction but turned to Marxist politics instead. Like the sons of many Hindu landlords who'd purchased their land from the British, he embraced communism when he realised that the feudal privilege setting him apart from the Muslim peasants was no longer tenable. But just as these communists dreamed of a classless society, the very class struggle of which they'd been a part, that of peasants against landlords, was getting overlaid with a religious conflict between Muslims and Hindus.

The state of Bangladesh hadn't been created yet. It was called East Bengal and formed part of Pakistan, where the Communist Party had been banned since 1947, right after the partition from India, for trying to seize power through a military coup. The party members had gone into hiding and begun to work clandestinely, including Boro Jethu, who'd been a member since the days of British rule.

As far back as Baba could remember, he'd always seen his brother on the run. Boro Jethu would appear out of nowhere in the dead of the night and enter the house by climbing over the wall. A police patrol would be after him. Eventually, another party member betrayed his trust, and he got caught. He ended up spending a total of fifteen years in prison.

During his first imprisonment, Boro Jethu translated a book called *Numbers: The Language of Science*. Like all communists in Bengal, he was obsessed with science. Science was their new religion. They'd left their idols behind to worship it. Whenever they discussed socialism, they inserted the word "scientific" before it. "Scientific socialism is our goal," they said.

After his release, Boro Jethu took up a job as a maths teacher at a high school. When he played with his mole, mathematical problems would get solved in the blink of an eye. You see, solving those problems was of great importance to him. If science was his religion, mathematics was his hymn. He practised it fervently and found great recognition as a teacher. But this new life proved just as fleeting as his former one. In the 1960s, Ayub Khan, the military ruler of Pakistan, had him arrested once again on charges of treason, and he was sent to a labour camp.

When he got out again, Boro Jethu decided to emigrate to neighbouring India; like me, he no longer felt welcome in his own homeland. India, of course, had been partitioned on the basis of religion—Pakistan for the Muslims and India for the Hindus. In a twist of fate as cruel as it was ironic, Boro Jethu had to revert to his religious identity to find a place in India since his political identity prevented him from staying in Pakistan.

My uncle was quite old when Stephen Hawking published *A Brief History of Time*. He'd become a lawyer in India, but the book filled him with such passion that he started studying physics once again and even translated it into Bengali.

After Boro Jethu passed away, my family commissioned a portrait of him—but his mole was nowhere to be seen. It was as if the person on the canvas couldn't come to life; the rest of the portrait was useless in the absence of the mole. It reminds me of a Bengali story about two lovers. One day, the man discovers that his lover's mole is no longer there. "There's no mole under her left eye," he says. "Oh, where did that mole disappear to? For the ten years of our love, the entirety of that woman's beauty resided in that mole!"

A Bowl of Milk

Fulkumari's visits are becoming more and more frequent, and she tolerates my presence for longer stretches of time. Sometimes, she comes very close before scuttling away, exhibiting many of her miraculous skills right in front of me. Her demeanour is that of a lady who has been kind enough to take in a castaway like me. As a rule, I place her food and water at a designated breakfast spot right after I wake up. She makes sure to lick the plate clean every day, but I've never been able to catch her in the act. It's something clandestine for her; it seems she's made a vow not to let anyone see her feasting.

"We may be going through this plague together," I start, hoping my voice will draw her out, "but there's so much—famines, war—that I've seen in this life without you."

The first time I had to flee my country was long ago, in 1971, during the civil war that separated Bangladesh from Pakistan. I was four years old, and my memory of the time is a patchwork. Some of the images are as vivid as if I were seeing them today, some of them I reconstructed with the help of Ma and others, and some are like broken shards, fragments of which I seem to be the only witness, unable to ascertain whether they're imagined or real.

Right before the war, riots broke out between the Bengalis and the Bihari Muslims who'd come to East Pakistan after the partition of India, and who mostly worked as labourers in shipyards and rail factories. Bihari neighbourhoods were besieged in several cities, and their inhabitants brutally massacred, by Bengali mobs made up of Muslims and Hindus alike. But at the time, Ma used to say that the Biharis had simply attacked the Hindus.

"Didn't other Muslims try to stop them?" I asked her.

"Of course they did," she said. "They even sheltered the victims."

Civil War

One of those people, Ma told me, was Mr. Khan, at whose house we found refuge when the Bengali-Bihari riots broke out in Bogra. This wealthy and respected gentleman also owned a cinema hall—the Marina Cinema Hall—which was managed by a Hindu, a very close family friend of ours. We used to call him Pishemoshai—Uncle. In fact, to be precise, the word denotes the husband of one's father's sister. Such distinctions are crucial in Bengali culture, where families extend like intricate networks and all relations carry different names, identities, and even stereotypes, while English bluntly subsumes them under one generic word.

Mr. Khan took us in—both our family and Pishemoshai's—at his magnificent courtyard house, protected by a wall. He stood watch all night with a gun outside the door, aided only by the occasional sip of alcohol. Intoxicated as he was, would he have been able to aim properly if the situation actually called for it? That remains a mystery to this day. In any case, we were fortunate. I don't know if it was out of fear of getting shot or the gravitas of Mr. Khan's name, but the rioters never came for us.

Shortly afterwards, the Pakistani army intervened, siding with the Biharis and triggering the massive Bengali resistance that eventually resulted in the separation of Bangladesh from Pakistan. The inhabitants of Bogra besieged the small Pakistani military contingent in its camp on the outskirts of the city. Reinforcements coming in from neighbouring Rangpur were constantly repelled, and Bogra remained free for about a month. But eventually, the Pakistani forces broke the resistance and recaptured the city.

Like many Hindus, we fled amidst a deluge of bullets. Bulbuli and I were still too little to walk long distances, but we didn't want to be held in a grown-up's arms either. So, a young man named Hari, one of our neighbours, put us in a basket that he balanced on his head. Scorched by the sun, drenched in the rain, and covered in mud, we made our way through the forest. Sometimes, all of us had to suck in our breaths and hide underwater. We waded through a sea of blood, tears, and maddening fear, running from village to village.

There's one particular incident that stands out, flashing like an ember in my memory. We're sitting on the veranda of a house. In front of us, there's a tea shop, where the boiling milk in a pot is bubbling over. The sweet smell wafts over to us. Our throats parched, Bulbuli and I turn to Ma with pleading eyes, tears spilling down our cheeks. Ma understands, takes up a tiny bowl, and goes over to the shop. But the shopkeeper chases her away with his hand, as if swatting away a fly. On that day, I vowed not to cry or beg my parents for anything ever again. I felt the pain that a mother must feel when she can't even offer her children a tiny bowl of milk.

Our journey took us out of Bogra, through the town of Joypurhat, across the border at Hili, and, finally, into India. When we arrived on Indian soil at long last, Baba heaved a sigh of relief before turning his sad gaze back to the path behind him. Perhaps he was telling himself that he might never get a chance to see his motherland again.

Millions fled to India just like us. Many had relatives there, but these people, unwilling to help their loved ones, pretended not to recognise their faces. Stories of such tragedies used to go around the refugee camps. Baba's elder sister was in a camp with her husband and their two sons. My oldest paternal uncle, who'd already settled in India, came to pick them up. My aunt's younger son, around my age and probably no stranger to those camp stories, asked his mother with frightened eyes what would become of them if her brother didn't accept them as his own.

My life at my relatives' place was not much better than at the refugee camp. Although I can't recall it myself, Ma tells me that my father's younger brother used to brutally beat me because I was an obstinate child. Deserted as I am by memory, the question haunts me to this day: just what kind of obstinacy could prompt an adult to constantly beat up a four-year-old refugee child?

From time to time, some young men from Bogra came to visit us in India. They seemed unperturbed by the war: not a single hair on their bodies was grazed. I was astounded—I'd always been told of brave young men leaving for the battlefields and fighting fearlessly for their country.

"These men are young and healthy," I said to Ma. "Why don't they go to war like the others?"

Ma chuckled. "They don't have the heart to fight and die."

Nirman Haji's Place

After nine months, scaling a mountain of lost lives, Bangladesh finally shook off the occupation. The Pakistani army had launched attacks on several cities in India for supporting Bangladeshi freedom fighters. These attacks gave India an excuse to directly involve itself in the conflict, leading to a humiliating defeat for Pakistan. But even though India appeared as a saviour at the time, its involvement only heralded another chapter of outside rule, even more pernicious than that of the Pakistanis. We'd called in the wolf to drive away the dogs.

During the war, our house had been occupied by a Muslim League leader. His name was Nirman; upon his return from the Hajj pilgrimage, everyone had taken to calling him Nirman Haji, including himself. After we fled the country, he'd taken a piece of white chalk and written the following sentence on our wall: *Yeh Nirman Haji ka muqam hai*—this is Nirman Haji's place. Urdu was the language of power at the time, so even though his native tongue was Bengali, he'd marked our home in Urdu.

I'd seen Nirman Haji around as a child; he was a slight, old man, always clad in the simple attire of a *panjabi* on top of a *lungi* when he passed by our house on his way to the mosque. It will always be a mystery to me how he could occupy his own neighbours' house during a time of war. As a child, I often used to tell myself that when I grew up, I'd take him to account, but I never got the chance. While I was at medical college, I received the news of his death. Be that as it may, Nirman Haji's reign over our house didn't last long. It was taken over by the Razakars, a local militia collaborating with the Pakistani army. They transformed it into a camp and a storehouse for all the goods they stole from neighbouring homes.

When we returned after the war, our refugee life finally coming to an end, we found out that our entire house had been burnt down by the Razakars before their retreat. Seeing our house like that is the memory that burns the brightest in my mind. The separate kitchen in our back yard was all that remained, and that was where our life began anew. The walls were covered in dark carbon soot from the firewood used for cooking. The coating was so thick that it was impossible to take off the entirety of that unyielding layer, so we just painted over it with lime. As the black of the carbon mingled with the white of the lime, our living quarters assumed a strange, gloomy, greyish colour.

Searching through the charred remains of what was once our sanctuary, we discovered that not everything was lost. Precious items, overlooked by the Razakars, gleamed through the ashes in quiet defiance. Many of these treasures were quickly reclaimed by our neighbours, but two significant pieces remained unspoken for: a magnificently decorated bed and an old, sturdy refrigerator. The bed, with its intricate carvings whispering tales of a different era, became the centrepiece of our rebuilt bedroom, while the refrigerator, a relic of resilience, stood proudly in our kitchen. They were no longer mere objects, but symbols of our perseverance and the complex layers of history and survival that our family would continue to weave into the fabric of our renewed existence.

I often used to rummage through the huge pile of ashes left over from the burned house. What I found the most fascinating were the charred remains of books, given a short lease on life by the moisture they'd soaked up outside. Most of them were law books—my grandfather was a famous lawyer, and his office in the house had been full of them, stacked on towering shelves all around. It seemed like the books were the same as they'd always been, save for the surfaces of the pages that had all been burnt black. The ink of the letters used to gleam through the blackened pages, and we could distinctly make out all the words. Of course, these books had to be handled with the utmost care; it wouldn't be long before their brittle pages came crumbling down.

That pile of ashes was the perfect spot for a treasure hunt. Once, I discovered a swan made of glass in it. The fire had melted off a portion of its neck and twisted it in such a charming way that it was no less a work of art, even in its disfigured form. On another lucky day, I found a golden, metallic mass. It turned out to be my grandfather's beloved watch. All the gold on it had melted and coalesced into a lump. Instead of exchanging it for money to cover our expenses, we used it to make a pair of earrings for Ma.

During the devastating wave of poverty that washed over the country after the war, we didn't even have sandals to wear on our feet. But the shoemakers of Bangladesh were creative. They started making sandals out of car tires and tubes—footwear that didn't decay. They were named *akshay*—indestructible. Although these sandals never decayed, they certainly did fall apart at some point. I don't remember how long we kept wearing them, but their memory will always be indestructible in our generation's mind.

The Leader Who Failed Maths

It isn't just my own memory of those days that has proven to be unreliable. After the war ended, an iconic photograph appeared in the dailies of the newly independent Bangladesh, depicting corpses of people shot in rickshaws, presented as evidence of the cruelty inflicted by the Pakistani army as it tried to suppress the Bangladeshi independence movement. I dimly remember asking myself as a child what these people were doing in rickshaws if the Pakistani army had actually attacked in the dead of the night as we'd been told. Later, I found out that the photo really depicted the bodies of Biharis killed by Bengalis.

There was another image that made the newspapers back then, apparently showing a soldier examining a man's genitalia. Again, this was supposed to illustrate the malice of Pakistani soldiers identifying Hindus by whether they were circumcised. However, the soldier in the photo was in fact from the Indian army that had supported Bangladeshi independence. He wasn't examining the man's genitalia but searching for concealed weapons in his *lungi*. These revelations made me question the veracity of the accounts of those who claimed to have witnessed the war firsthand. And today, decades later, when I go online, I can still see the same photos being used to distort history in the exact same way.

During the war, Sheikh Mujib, the political leader of the independence movement, was imprisoned in Pakistan. When he was finally released, he flew to London on a Red Cross plane, where he met a BBC reporter and asked him about the death toll in the war. The reporter told him there was no confirmed figure and gave him an estimate of around three *lakh*, meaning three hundred thousand. But Sheikh Mujib had never been very good at maths: even his college tutors later confirmed that he used to regularly fail his exams. And so, the three *lakh* became three million.

Three million dead in nine months of low-intensity guerrilla warfare followed by just one week of full-scale war! And all this at a time when the population of Bangladesh was around seventy-five million, with over ten million having fled to India. Sheikh Mujib later set up a commission to investigate the matter, and it came back with a number closer to thirty thousand. But by then, the three million were such a part of the country's founding myth that he refused to accept the finding. Today, the number is so sacred that it's protected by law—dare to question it, and off you go to jail, for a minimum sentence of fourteen years.

The final irony was that the violence of the civil war was actually genocidal, on both sides—but because of the fantastically exaggerated death toll, the United Nations has never accepted any claims of genocide.

Dadhichi's Bones

On the empty streets of Paris, those whose absence I notice the most are the *clochards*. They can no longer be found playing their soulful tunes in the metro, hawking trinkets on the roads, or simply sitting and begging at a convenient spot, like the woman at my supermarket's entrance used to do. The *clochards* lived each day without the safety of stable jobs, without the promise of a single coin. How are they surviving the lockdown, I wonder? Have they found shelter in a state-paid hotel, just as Fulkumari has with me? Are they fed, as she is by me?

As a child, I saw countless hungry people begging for food; their skeletal, almost lifeless bodies, on the streets and on our doorstep, haunt my memories to this day. The famine broke out in 1974, two years after the supposed liberation of Bangladesh. Neither food nor clothing were to be found anywhere, not because they didn't exist, but because, as Amartya Sen so compellingly showed, they didn't reach the people due to the corruption and mismanagement of the Sheikh Mujib regime. Even during the famine, one man's plight was another's opportunity: grabbing whatever weapons had been abandoned by the Pakistani army upon its retreat, people looted shops, destroyed homes, and stole whatever they could, simply to amass more wealth.

As even our previous, meagre rations were cut down, my family had to survive on basics: rice, potatoes, lentils. At school, we were given some high-protein biscuits, but we couldn't eat them due to their strange flavour. I realise today they were mixed with cheese—a taste entirely absent from my childhood diet. And we were the lucky ones. Others had to quell their hunger with the most undesirable of foods, like sweet potatoes and taro root, or things that weren't really foods at all: rice husk, rice starch, various leaves and herbs. There were even those who gnawed at the soles of leather shoes.

Fulkumari

Train stations became home to the masses who poured in from the countryside in search of something—anything—to eat, and it was almost impossible not to step on a lifeless, or nearly lifeless, body while getting on or off the train. Here's how a journalist from the time described the scene:

> A starving, nearly-dead man lay on the platform, rubbing his chest and licking up the vomited rice left behind by a passenger. In Bogra, people tried to survive on the same diet as ducks and hens. Among those who survived cholera, some took their own lives or helped their relatives do the same.

I'm reminded of our previous great famine, the Bengal Famine of 1943, once again born out of a power struggle at the top, combined with a monstrous negligence for the lives of those at the bottom. Like the rest of India, Bengal was under British rule, and in their effort to prevent the Japanese army crossing over from Burma, the British requisitioned all available river boats. They cared little for the fact that, in doing so, they fatally compromised Bengal's internal food supply, which was completely dependent on boat transport. Much later, the Indian poet Premendra Mitra summed up the outcome of this policy:

> In the roads, I see the skeletons of the children who died without the luxury of drinking from their mother's breasts. Were Dadhichi's bones stronger than theirs?

A revered Hindu sage, Dadhichi is best known for his ultimate sacrifice, when he willingly gave up his life so that Indra could use his holy bones to forge the Vajra, the celestial thunderbolt with which he defeated the demon Vritra, who fought to usurp the gods' rightful place. Sometimes I can't help but wonder—was Indra's rule of the heavens worth the sage's sacrifice?

And in my childhood, once again, the people of Bengal's cities were awaking to the blood-curdling screams of the starving. The wails of an unfortunate soul usually lasted no more than a day; the next morning, those who'd run around the streets bellowing were found crumpled up in a corner, completely still and quiet. Beggars wouldn't even ask for rice, only rice water, and they'd quarrel over that as well. Only three years before, amidst war and bloodshed, the country had gained its so-called independence, receiving a map of its own. Now, unable to withstand his own searing hunger, the poet Rafique Azad wrote, "Give me rice, you bastard. Or I will eat up the map!"

Sometimes I can't help but wonder—what exactly did we get liberated from? People lay down their lives struggling against power. But if they win, they suddenly find themselves on the other side of power. And what's more, they know what power can do, how it can be abused, better than anyone else. When Nazi Germany was defeated by the Allied powers in the Second World War, Allied soldiers raped hundreds of thousands of German women. Tell me, then—what did Europe achieve by defeating fascism if that victory had to be celebrated with rape?

Baba's Final Journey

Fragmented sleep and unsettling dreams seem to foreshadow a tumultuous day. I wake up to the sound of Fulkumari, my usually serene companion, scuttling around in distress. Her strange behaviour strengthens the sense of foreboding.

Checking my phone, I'm gripped by a wave of panic. Missed calls from my brother, my sister, my mother. Social media flooded with frantic messages. The first one I open tells me the whole story: my father has collapsed, fallen unconscious, and been rushed to the hospital.

I call my brother, with trembling hands. He's already on his way from Dhaka to Bogra.

"Baba had a stroke," he says, his voice taut with worry. "What should we do?"

As the oldest son—my brother is twelve years my junior—and the only doctor in the family, the decision falls to me, even in Paris, even confined to my tiny apartment where all I can do is helplessly watch from afar.

"Talk to the doctor. See if you can have him transferred to Dhaka."

His condition has been deteriorating for some time. Symptoms of Alzheimer's were becoming ever more evident—his memories slipping away, recent events fading into oblivion while the distant past became his new reality. He no longer recognised our home, incessantly questioning my mother, convinced it was a foreign place. "It's not ours," he would insist. Was this dementia, or a stark reminder of the ephemeral nature of our material possessions?

I know, by training and instinct, that it'll be very hard for him to come back from this. It hits me with a clinical sort of clarity that I'll probably never see him again.

Baba was seen by many in his life, despite being a natural introvert. Trained as an electrical engineer, he realised after a short stint in public service that this wasn't the path for him. It was on stage that his heart truly belonged. Once we were back home after the civil war, he founded a theatre troupe, surrounding himself with a group of young Bogran thespians. He was one of many people marked by the war who went into theatre and film at the time, seeking to give meaning to their experiences through art. Many war heroes, in fact, found it easier on the stage of theatre than the stage of politics to make sense of the world, the war, and the woes of the budding nation.

Baba's troupe quickly drew attention, growing into a cultural beacon in Bogra. At the age of fourteen, I became their touring photographer, travelling across the country with them, attending their shows, and watching them from backstage. The mundane mechanics behind the scenes sometimes dimmed the enchantment of the performances for me, but the spirit of solidarity on the road, singing our songs while travelling to our next venue, will stay with me forever.

The troupe's first rehearsal space was on the top floor of a cinema. I was instantly drawn to the projection room. New movies wouldn't come often, maybe once a month, but whenever they did, I'd watch them from up there, captivated by the scent of the film reels and intrigued by the projection process that involved two separate machines.

Baba and I bonded over our love of movies, and as the years went by, he often asked me to send him certain films. Slowly, together, we built an archive of classics, collecting hundreds of them—English, Iranian, Russian. Baba was the secretary general of the Bangladeshi-Soviet Friendship Society in Bogra, and as such, he was sent many films by the Russians. We'd watch these together, sometimes with Ma, sometimes just the two of us, on the society's projector, which we stored at home since the society had no office of its own.

He was also an avid reader. After starting work in Dhaka, I made an arrangement with a major bookstore: anything my father ordered, they'd send to him, and I would cover the cost. Baba used to read deep into the night, and so, he'd set up a bed in his study so as not to disturb Ma. The room was a testament to his love for books, its walls lined with beautifully archived volumes, each meticulously tagged.

At that point, our lives had already drifted apart. In 2018, despite Baba's declining health, we took a family trip to India for a wedding. I had no inkling at the time, but this would be our last trip together. A year later, I was in exile.

Police harassment became a regular feature of life at our Bogra home after I left. Even as he became more and more ill, Baba was interrogated over and over again by the police and unscrupulous journalists who gained access to our home pretending to be his former students and went on to publish interviews with him in which he was barely coherent.

As much as I regret that I cannot be with him now, I cannot regret the actions that led me to leave my country. Many people questioned me, noting the risks to which I exposed my own family. I always simply responded that silence in the face of fascist rule was immoral. I never sat down to discuss my choices with Baba. But Ma told me the only thing I ever needed to know: "That's what I taught him to do," he'd once said to her.

In recognition of Baba's cultural work, the government eventually granted his troupe a prime piece of land in the heart of Bogra for their theatre. Yet this gift soon became a source of conflict in the troupe. Some young members who'd once revered Baba sought to seize the land for themselves. They turned against him, threatened him, and ultimately took control of the property, using it to construct an office building. This betrayal shattered Baba's dreams. He tried to start a new troupe, but without the same energy and support, it never gained prominence. Eventually, he shifted his focus to studying and got a law degree, though his heart never left the stage.

The person who took over the theatre land had been a valiant freedom fighter, renowned for his bravery in resisting the Pakistani army and maintaining Bogra's freedom for a month. Ironically, the same person was also implicated in the notorious central bank heist in Bogra, where the vault was looted to fund the Kolkata government in exile. But once those people got their hands on the money, they lavishly spent it on luxury, entertainment, and sexual gratification. Somehow, the supposed morality of the civil war didn't trickle down into their everyday lives.

I call my brother and uncle multiple times each day, trying to find the best way to proceed with Baba's treatment. Eventually, we have an air ambulance take him to Dhaka, to the best hospital in Bangladesh. They find a source of continuous bleeding in his brain. The culprit is the blood thinner he's been taking for his heart condition ever since 2015, when an irregular heartbeat led to the discovery that some of the arteries in his heart were partially clogged. The bleeding in his brain has likely been going on for one or two years. There's nothing the doctors can do. We fly him back to Bogra.

One morning, my brother calls.

"Did you hear the news?"

There's only one piece of news that warrants such an introduction. Baba has died in his sleep. His journey is complete.

Religion would have us believe that we never truly die; that our inner selves leave this mortal body and return to eternity. Fairy tales can be more comforting sometimes, telling us that those we lose, composed of celestial matter, rise up to become stars guiding us from the night sky. I already know I will look for Baba up there, but ever the rationalist, he gave us his final guidance long before he died. Refusing to be cremated as per custom, he told us that he wished for his body to be donated to medical research. We honour his request.

I learn from the papers that after Baba's passing, all the neighbourhood shops closed in his memory, in silent tribute to a man who once brought such a vibrant culture to the city. Though celebrated in death, Baba was unable to achieve his full potential in life. His story is a reminder how we often fail to support those who truly dare to challenge us while they're still among us. In death, when they're no longer able to disrupt our complacency, we have no trouble laying flowers on their graves.

Baba had a day job, of course; he was a high school teacher, and it was here, perhaps, that he left his greatest mark. At first, he taught geometrical and technical drawing, along with applied electrical engineering. Eventually, these subjects were deemed unnecessary and removed from the curriculum. At that point, Baba made a seamless transition to teaching Bengali literature and Arabic. One of his students, who went on to become the principal of Bogra Medical College, later recalled how Baba, a Hindu from a Brahman family, had embraced the role of teaching Islam to Muslim children like himself. His deep love and respect for knowledge and culture, no matter their origin, was reflected in the love and respect his students held for him.

Growing Pains

Ramu

I go out shopping a few days in a row, slithering down the streets like a lonely, listless python that only moves when searching for food. Outside the supermarket, I take my place in a long queue of people, each of them waiting with a patience born of necessity. The line extends like a weary river, its end lost in the distance. Hours pass slowly, almost painfully, as people enter the store in a measured, single file. So lengthy is this vigil that often, just as my turn seems within reach, it's already time for the store to close. Yet on those days when luck smiles faintly upon me, and I make it across the threshold, I'm greeted by yawning shelves.

This dreary routine takes me straight back to my childhood in Bogra, where I often waited outside the ration shop in exactly the same way. Even after the famine was overcome—a surprisingly easy feat once the Sheikh Mujib regime was toppled in August 1975—the lower and middle class families of Bangladesh still had to survive on rations. Each family had a ration card that determined its monthly allocation and slowly used it up over the course of the month. Rice, wheat, sugar, and oil were the regularly rationed items. Sometimes, we also got soap and powdered milk. And on Eid, we got *semai*, the festive wheat vermicelli.

The ration shop was near our house, and since the prices were fixed and there was no room for bargaining, Ma often sent me over on my own although I wasn't even ten years old. The shop manager was a certain Zainul Abedin, a namesake of the famous Bangladeshi painter, but to my child's imagination, he *was* the painter; I'd never seen a photo of the man, and surely he couldn't be living off painting alone?

Even when I bought the other rationed items, I never got the rice because it stank and always had insects in it. The wheat had to be taken to the mill, where a pungent smell and the dust

Fulkumari

of the fine flour in the air made it hard to breathe. Still, I loved going there, because whatever husks were left behind after the wheat had been threshed, I was allowed to take home to feed my pet goat, Ramu.

We didn't actually own Ramu; a friend of Baba's had asked us to look after her on the condition that we got to keep her milk. A huge, calm goat with brown fur, Ramu was quite an introvert. Her favourite spot was under the jackfruit tree in our yard, and she hardly ever left it. She didn't make much noise and wasn't friendly with most people except for me. When Ramu came to live with us, she was alone, but soon afterwards, she gave birth to a pair of kids. They had to share her milk with us—sometimes up to two litres a day.

It occurred to me much later that in depriving the kids of their mother's milk, we were actually practising "non-violence" of the kind preached by Mahatma Gandhi. Gandhiji was a vegetarian, but for some reason, he found it acceptable to drink goat's milk, which he mixed with garlic juice. He preferred goat's milk because he thought that cow's milk led to sexual arousal, which he treated with more caution than the political arousal he caused.

Mahadev Desai, Gandhiji's secretary, used to personally select the goat who was to provide him with his daily supply of milk. Each day, Mahadev would line up the goats and inspect them with a grave expression on his face. He'd reject the goats that couldn't withstand his gaze and lowered their heads, deeming them "liars," and select the goat that held his stare without looking away.

Apart from the milk, Gandhiji made a point of only eating fourteen *paisas*' worth of vegetables a day, which basically meant a single one. But there were only fifteen sorts he'd eat, and they weren't easy to find. Also, he didn't appreciate the monotony of having the same vegetable every day. So, Mahadev would keep note of all the vegetables Gandhiji had eaten, and by eleven o'clock each day—an hour before Gandhiji's lunchtime—would give instructions about which one needed to be procured. This daily performance of austerity was pretty expensive indeed.

The collective anxiety that has gripped Paris under lockdown has led to its own excesses masked as austerity. Driven by an unseen dread, the masses fill their homes with more than they could ever need. The act of shopping is no longer a mere indulgence or even a quest for necessities; it has become a race against an invisible clock, each of its ticks echoing the deep-seated fears of our shared human experience.

In this landscape of scarcity, fresh fruit and vegetables are the rarest of all treasures, and people plan their purchase with a meticulousness that would put Mahadev to shame. Their presence on the shelves is as ephemeral as the morning dew, vanishing almost as soon as it appears. Rumours from afar tell of an even stranger shortage—in the United States, not a single roll of toilet paper is to be found. The logic eludes me; how could such a simple item combat the might of the plague?

As it did when I was a child, my shopping quest extends beyond my own needs. Instead of wheat for Ramu, I now search for rat food, a small offering for my friend Fulkumari—but to no avail. While hosting an array of cat food, the store seems oblivious to the needs of a tiny rat. I scan every corner, every shelf, seeking but not finding. A sobering realisation dawns on me: the boundaries of human compassion have been drawn at the feet of the cat. The humble rat, despite its simple needs, remains overlooked, an outcast in this hierarchy of affection.

The Sliced Egg

I just got off the phone with my friend Olivera. He's a dentist, originally from Cuba, who lives with his family near my apartment in Jules Joffrin. Olivera used to work in Dhaka and was on the expert panel at a seminar where I spoke on the Cuban healthcare system. Our friendship blossomed over shared market trips, cooking sessions, and meals. His wife, Sabine, was from France, and she developed a delicious fusion of Bangladeshi and French cuisine, while Oliveira mastered the art of the mojito. After my precipitous escape from Bangladesh and arrival in Paris, I gradually started getting in touch with old friends and acquaintances—I'd spent five months underground and had no idea anymore who was doing what. That's when I learned that Olivera, Sabine, and their little son Gael had moved to Paris.

Before the lockdown, I often visited Olivera and his family for evenings filled with laughter and games with Gael. And whenever we sat down to eat, I was amazed by the spread before us. After a year of life as a refugee, I was no longer accustomed to such opulence. My astonishment must have been evident, but thankfully, Sabine was usually too busy to notice. I'm reminded of the Bengali writer Syed Mujtaba Ali, who was similarly overwhelmed by a masterful culinary display during his time in Afghanistan. Reading his surprise as concern, the cook reassured him: "There's more in the kitchen!"

Throughout my childhood, I stayed skinny, thin like a reed, malnourished, and sick. The protein in our diet was mostly made up of pulses and, on rare occasions, a piece of meat or fish. Once in a while, we were granted the luxury of an egg—though never a whole one. Eggs were always sliced neatly down the middle with a thread, and Bulbuli and I were each allotted one half.

At some point, we were invited over for dinner by one of Baba's students. Her father was quite a wealthy man by the standards of the time, and my eyes became glued to the dining table, darting from one mouthwatering dish to another. What bewildered me the most, however, were the eggs—so many, and none of them sliced in half! I still remember how the lady of the house insisted on serving Ma a second helping of a whole egg, even as she kept firmly refusing. On the way home, I asked Ma in amazement if it were really possible for someone to have two eggs in one sitting!

Another day, Baba and I were walking past the famous Azad Bakery in the Saptapadi Market. It was the oldest bakery in Bogra, but now it was on the brink of closure, crowded out by newer, fancier shops that had lured away its custom. As we were passing by, we were drawn into the shop by the last patrons of this fading glory. Their invitation, extended with warmth and a mix of respect and obligation, led us to an experience far from our daily struggles.

I distinctly remember the old, filament light bulbs that bathed the dark maroon shelves in a reddish hue. The shop was small and normally had standing room only, but since it was barely operational, two or three people had made themselves comfortable inside on makeshift chairs. Baba was offered a chair, and I was handed a cold, fizzy drink in a bottle, cool to the touch, and a slice of cake. To me, this was more than a mere snack—it was a portal to a new world of sensations.

The cake had some pieces of sweet fruit inside, which I later discovered weren't really fruit at all. They'd boiled bottle gourd, a tasteless vegetable, in sugar syrup to create those fruit-like pieces. What a deception indeed! The cold fizz of the drink was a delight I'd never experienced before, its effervescence a dance of flavours. Yet it was the straw, an unfamiliar tool, that posed a fateful challenge. I bit down on it in my eagerness, crushing it and turning my enjoyment of the drink into a struggle. I suppose I could have drunk straight from the bottle, but I somehow felt it was inappropriate, and I was too embarrassed to ask for a second straw. In the end, I had to leave most of the drink untouched, and that first bottle of fizzy drink I tasted in my life has been taunting me ever since.

Upon leaving the bakery, Baba said something that would forever shape my understanding of our place in the world. "What just happened, Pinku," he said, "might well have been a rare luxury. Life has its ways to remind us of our place, and such luxuries might not easily find their way back to us." When I heard those words, it dawned on me for the first time that perhaps, the hardships Baba had endured weren't just his own, but a legacy that I might have to bear throughout my own life.

As I look out my window and down the empty street that leads to Olivera's home, so close and yet so elusive now, I can't help but ponder just how right my father was. Olivera's friendship—so easily taken for granted during our time together in Dhaka, so easily lost when I went underground, and so miraculously regained in Paris. Sabine's delicious cooking—so casually consumed in Dhaka, so magnificent after a year on the run, and so completely out of reach in these pandemic days. Luxuries indeed.

Liquid Symphony

The morning light fails to show its face through the clouds that crowd the sky. Darkness persists all around. Fulkumari watches from her corner, her tiny eyes reflecting the grey Parisian skies, her presence subtle and reassuring. Perhaps she senses my nostalgia, understanding it in her own, silent way. She scuttles across the room, her tiny paws barely making a sound on the floor, her movements hesitant yet curious, exploring this foreign world that has become her home.

She pauses, lifting her gaze to the skies. Monsoon is on the cusp, ready to cloak Paris in its gentle embrace. Here, the rain falls with a softness, a tender caress compared to the formidable downpours of Bangladesh where rain wields power, where thunder cracks like celestial whips across the sky, and clouds roar their presence, instilling awe and fear. In Paris, the rain is a quiet lullaby, a soothing serenade that whispers of renewal and calm. But in Bangladesh, it's an orchestra of nature's raw force, a reminder of the earth's unbridled energy and the resonant voice of the heavens.

During my childhood monsoon nights, I would count the raindrops while falling asleep, listening to them strike the tin roof above. Each raindrop is a note of music, the roof its instrument, and together they compose a liquid symphony. The sound of a large, bulbous droplet falling haphazardly on the roof is completely different from the continuous string of raindrops that slide down the tin, weaving a persistent ribbon of sound.

As the rain subsides and the skies take a breath, a new symphony begins. Droplets once hidden within the leaves of the guava tree that towers over the roof embark on a gentle descent. Some land on other guava leaves, soft and velvety to the touch, that cradle the water carefully, while others land on the hard leaves of the jackfruit tree, cascading from one to the next in a playful dance. Some droplets reach the earth, mingling with the soil, while others take a spirited leap from these taller trees onto the taro root leaves beneath, their landing echoing softly like the beat of a drum, a quiet postlude to the storm.

The massive taro leaves serve as our makeshift umbrellas. I marvel at them, a timely monsoon blessing, flourishing just when we need them most, as if bestowed by the heavens to give us shelter. In the mornings, I often find myself irresistibly drawn to tasting the raindrops lingering on the leaves. The soft allure of the guava leaves is too strong to resist, tempting me to take a bite, only to find their flavour disappointingly bitter.

With my eyes closed, I see villagers under their taro leaves, making their way to the barns and ponds. Perhaps some are carrying breakfast, wrapped in cloth, to ploughmen working in waterlogged fields. Today, the farmers have to eat their food in the rain, while the fishermen do the same sitting in the hulls of their boats. The earthy aroma of soil mingled with rain fills the air, while cows lower their heads, their fur standing upright. From the nearby barns echo the soft calls of calves seeking their mothers.

In the corner of a yard, ducks quack loudly, demanding their release from the coop, while the chickens huddle in silence, finding refuge beneath the little granary huts, and the pigeons stay perfectly still. Someone is cooking, ribbons of smoke spiralling through a straw roof, blending with the clouds above. Across the river, the wild wind frolics freely in the fields, making them sway ever so gracefully—a sight to behold.

The fishermen return, bearing baskets of fresh hilsa slung from bamboo strips over their shoulders. The unique fragrance of the fish fills the air of Bangladesh, a sweet aroma that marks the rainy day. I pity those who've never savoured this fish—its taste seems to hail from another realm entirely. In the West, they struggle with its bony texture. There's a culinary creation known as smoked hilsa, a boneless dish, yet few possess the skill to prepare it. Perhaps we're reluctant to share this exquisite delight with the world, fearing it might expose the cherished secrets of our heritage and strip away our simple joy.

There are two scents that I absolutely adore. One is the sweet, intoxicating smell you get when you walk past a cowshed, and the other is the strangely suffocating scent that emanates from the soil when it welcomes the first drops of rain. As a child, I used to wait all year for the monsoon just so I could inhale that scent. In Bengali, it's called *soda gondho*, the earthy smell. I wasn't sure if any other language had a name dedicated to it, but then I learned of a place called Kannauj in Uttar Pradesh, where they use this scent to make a perfume known as *mitti ka attar*, the perfume of the soil. They only prepare this perfume during the rainy season. The smell of the rain as it kisses the earth somehow returns us to our roots. The children of the earth want to come closer to their mother by smelling like the fragrant soil itself.

My sky darkens as the rain carries the long-lost scent of Bangladesh's earth all the way to Paris. In the revered Sanskrit epic, the *Meghdut*, a soldier, cursed and exiled for a lapse in duty, speaks to the clouds, entreating them to carry his message of love to his wife. With delicate precision, he tells them of the journey they're about to undertake, and the sights they'll behold en route. His words, laden with pain and yearning, breathe life into the clouds, transforming them into silent bearers of his plight.

Here, under Parisian skies, the clouds drift differently. Even as I find myself whispering to them, they refuse to bear the weight of my sorrows and longing. Clouds have a soul, a spirit that can be cherished. That much was clear to Buddhadeva Bose, who translated the *Meghdut* into Bengali, but also to Baudelaire. *J'aime les nuages*, the French poet said, *les nuages qui passent... là-bas... là-bas... les merveilleux nuages*! I'm still waiting for the moment when I will perceive the clouds not merely as bearers of news, but as entities deserving of love.

Indifferent to the cloud-veiled skies, Fulkumari retreats to her cherished kitchen space, leaving me alone. Perhaps it'll rain more heavily at night, like it used to during my childhood days. Perhaps I'll wake up to see a newborn sun and a sanctified earth from which the plague has vanished. Perhaps, in this new light, I'll weave another tale for her, a refreshed story of my life born from the cleansing rains.

Thunder and the Coconut Tree

Fulkumari is afraid of thunder.

Darkness has gathered around the city once again, and the first droplets of rain have started to enter my apartment through the window. I have yet to see any kind of lightning accompanying Parisian rain. Just then, I hear thunder, for the very first time in Paris, and Fulkumari, who's been sitting pensively in her kitchen corner, surrenders to her instincts, her feet carrying her off faster than the wind.

As for myself, I'm transported back to my childhood, as I always am in times of rain and thunder.

Once again, it's the time of Durga Puja. Bulbuli and I are sitting on the back veranda, having our lunch. We can hear Baba walking up and down the front veranda, reciting the *Priyotomeshu* by Sukanta Bhattacharya, a communist poet who died at only twenty-one, a mere three months before the end of British colonial rule.

The poem captures the journey of a soldier whose service has spanned numerous battlefields and who is now beckoned back to the hearth of his home. He lists his lifelong wages as a warrior: in Tunisia, a crown of victory; amidst Italy's streets, bonds of friendship; in France, the wand of freedom; and, finally, in Burma, the longing for a homeland free from the affliction of colonial rule. In the concluding stanza, the soldier compares himself to a lamplighter: illuminating paths and byways wherever he goes, he finds his own abode shrouded in impenetrable shadows, a crushing darkness, unlit and profound.

Suddenly, my eyes widen as a massive, bright flame flashes right in front of me. I smell something burning, but I'm trapped in complete darkness, and I cannot hear a thing except for a strange, jingling sound. Then, I hear Bulbuli's scream, piercing the dark, bringing me back to my senses. I see Ma running over to us from the kitchen. Some people arrive and tell us they've seen a bolt of lightning strike our coconut tree, the one that towers over all the other trees in our yard. I look at it: it's still swaying gently in the breeze, reaching into the sky as if nothing has happened.

Bulbuli is still trembling when our parents take her inside. Ma fetches some tamarind that she's been ageing for a while and mixes it with water before giving it to my sister. The moon rises in the sky, lighting up everything below. Bulbuli doesn't eat anything all night. She's down with a fever. Delirious, she keeps repeating—Fire! Fire!

The next day, we notice that two branches of the coconut tree look misshapen, as if someone has twisted them. Whenever a crow comes and alights on a branch, it cracks, unable to bear the bird's weight. Throughout the day, branch after branch keeps cracking, hanging down from the tree as if by a thread. The coconut tree has protected us by embracing the thunderbolt, born amidst mighty clouds in the distant sky, finding respite in the earth after spending all its power on the tree in a mere instant.

Karna

I've taken care of several animals in my lifetime, but the pet I loved the most was a mongoose. I named him Karna, after the hero of the *Mahabharata*. Just like the warrior, abandoned by his mother as a child, our Karna's story began when he was discovered by a villager who used to frequent our home to sing in hopes of earning a modest offering of money or food. This kindhearted soul found Karna, vulnerable and alone, and in an act of rare compassion, brought him to our doorstep. With his hairy body and rapidly blinking red eyes, Karna easily could have been deemed terrifying. But his outward form concealed a truly good heart.

When Karna first came to our house, he was quite like myself, sickly and gaunt. But a couple of days of eating well, and he started to look much better. I got him the cheap pool barb fish from the market. At first, I let him gobble it up raw. But after some days, a foul odour began to emanate from his body. Ma advised me to boil the fish after coating it with salt and turmeric. I did as she said, and gradually, the unpleasant smell began to fade away. I had a peculiar relationship with Karna. It often seemed to me that he could understand what I was saying.

There was a hissing, croaking sound that Karna used to make—it was his signature call. I memorised it, too, and mimicked it whenever I called him. As soon as I made that sound, he'd appear faster than light. I'd hold out my right arm, and he'd jump up and wrap himself around it with all four limbs. Sometimes, when he was feeling particularly affectionate, he put his forearms around my neck and stayed there for a while. On such occasions, I carried his heavy body around as if we were mother and child. He never hurt me with his nails.

Beyond his prowess in battle, Karna the warrior was a paragon of generosity, willing to give up all that he owned, including his invincible armour, which he gave to a foe in disguise, fully aware that the act would strip him of its protective might. Like his namesake, our Karna possessed unparalleled instincts for self-protection, agility, and strength. And yet, he surrendered his armour to me, a mere human, a boy who'd won his trust.

One day, Karna was gone. Who would look for him? I ventured out, searching frantically all over the neighbourhood. I rummaged about the roots, trunks, and branches of trees; I looked through piles of bricks and wood; searched behind the bushes. I called for him: Karna! Karna? And I let out our signature call.

A few days later, Karna returned. One of his legs was broken. Someone had caught him and beaten him mercilessly before trapping him in a jug. After this ordeal, Karna wasn't the same anymore. He walked with a limp and refused to let anyone near. He never responded to my call or climbed in my lap again. Like his namesake, killed in battle after giving away his armour, Karna didn't survive for long after that. The unfair struggle had broken not only his leg, but also his heart. The trust he harboured for human beings was destroyed in the blink of an eye. Karna never hurt anyone in any way. But his unsightly appearance turned out to be enough of a crime. I learned the simplest reason for completely wiping out another's existence: "You're different. You're not like me."

Even today, I look for Karna in my dreams. I walk to the very end of our road, up to the Jaleshwari temple, after which our neighbourhood, Jaleshwaritala, is named. Jaleshwari is the local name for Mother Kali, and we live under her shade. She stands at the temple, a garland of heads in her hand, flowers around her neck, her tongue bitten. Shiva, her husband, lies beneath her foot. He's asleep. Kali is the mother of everything. Her name derives from *kal*, which signifies time, the cycle of creation and destruction. Once, her husband, Mahadeva, the supreme deity, dared to place himself in her way. Inadvertently, Kali stepped on him and, in a moment of embarrassment, bit her tongue.

Across the road from the temple is the dwelling of the idol sculptors. I'm familiar with every nook and cranny of this old, ruined shed, which also serves as the town *barowari*, the communal gathering place. It would have been easy had Karna been lost there. Next to the shed is a huge pond with a wide bank, its waters never rippling because they brim with hyacinths. When I reach it, the pond starts to swim before my eyes, as if turning into a huge river. I spot someone building an idol of Mother Durga, sculpting it from the mud on the bank. It is Pal, a sculptor we know very well. He comes around every year, once during Durga Puja and then during Saraswati Puja, to build the idols whose life is only as long as the festivals in their honour. But he doesn't recognise me.

"Which house are you from, boy?" he asks.

Which house am I from? "Karna's house," I say.

"Which Karna?"

"The Karna who got lost."

The shadow of a siris tree drapes over my head before leaning down to touch the idol. The elderly craftsman spreads his towel on the ground. A breeze washes over me. I lie down on the towel, and before I know it, I'm lulled into a deep sleep. A cat is standing there, perfectly still. "Quiet," he whispers, "be quiet."

Karna comes to me in my sleep. He curls up by my feet, the soft fur of his body caressing my skin. Pal the sculptor gently touches my forehead with his lean, mud-stained fingers. "Don't you ever get lost, little boy," he says.

How could I get lost? Even if there were no people around, Karna would always be there. He'd surely come to find me.

But finally, many years later, I did get lost after all. I left my homeland on foot, a small bag slung over my shoulder, tracing an unfamiliar border.

"Where are we going?" Karna whispered into my ear.

"I don't know," I said.

"We're getting lost again," Karna said. "But this time, we're both lost together."

That was when I learned what it truly meant to be lost. The banyan tree, the temple, Mother Kali biting her tongue, her husband Shiva fast asleep, the town *barowari*, the small field, the bank of the pond, the shade of the siris tree, the sculptor with his half-finished idol, and even my Karna know today—once you leave, you never return.

Interlude

The Divine in the Details

With human beings confined to their dwellings for several months now, the rest of nature has started taking over the earth again. Dolphins are back in the seas, fishes are playing about in the rivers, and the sky is getting clearer as carbon emissions disappear. All creatures are returning to their homes, be they cockroaches or worms, chameleons or snakes. Their ancestors must have resided here, and now they've come to reclaim their place.

Fulkumari also returns to my room. Lately, her courage has grown; she no longer runs away, even when I make a sudden move. I keep food and water in the kitchen for her every day. She finishes her meals regularly, though her dignity still prevents her from dining in my presence, so I'm not sure if she enjoys them alone or with her companion, whom I haven't seen again since our first encounter. Now, she scurries across the room, coming to a halt right in the middle. Her ears are upright again.

I close the book I've been reading and get up from my chair, moving in her direction, hoping to become better friends. But she pulls back once again; I suppose I still haven't fully earned her trust. Such an ungrateful one, isn't she? She takes the food I give her, she listens to my stories, and still, she doesn't confide in me. Of course, even in retreat, she makes sure to show off her bravery by shaking her ears and her tail. I can't decide if I should go back to reading or keep chasing her. But no, I can't see her anywhere now. She has disappeared, within a fraction of a second, like a flash of lightning.

I sit down to read once again. Invented by human beings, books can't be acquired straight from nature. We created them to store knowledge in the space enclosed between their two covers. Books are often revered among the educated elite, and being a book lover is considered a mark of distinction. However, I find myself questioning whether books are truly our companions.

Once we get hold of a book, we don't listen to people anymore. Listening is an art that needs to be mastered, but with a book in our hands, we assume that Gutenberg's printing press has handed us all the knowledge in the world. All we need to do now is read. It's alright if we don't talk to anyone; we can become wise just by reading, even if we have no firsthand knowledge of what we're reading about. But don't the illiterate know things too? And didn't our ancestors know things too, when the printing press wasn't even invented?

As we keep reading, our eyes grow more perceptive than our ears. When a bird chirps outside our window, we're unable to recognise it just by its call; we've been making our eyes do what our ears should have been doing. And yet, we probably wouldn't even recognise the bird by sight, because our eyes haven't been doing what they should, either. We have to look for a matching picture in a book or download an app on the phone to find out if the bird is a pigeon or a dove. Doves are everywhere in Paris; I learned to tell a dove from a pigeon only after I came here.

Older people today often complain that children are perpetually glued to mobile screens. Before our phones, we were just as engrossed in the pages of books, and still, reading books is praised while staring at a screen is frowned upon. Mobile screens actually engage more of our senses than books do, as they require us not only to read, but also to listen and watch. So, why the condemnation?

Fulkumari is back, but she's no longer alone. Her companion is by her side once again, reuniting the Kinnar-Mithun in my presence. I wonder what the significance of this portentous event might be. My friend seems different somehow, slower in her motions, less circumspect, moving across the floor in a ponderous, almost regal way. Side by side with her lover, cloaked in blue moonlight, she blossoms on the ground like a flower of mortal desire. Is that a divine tiara gracing her hair? Is it the crushed bark of a tree that colours her cheeks, or the floral pollen used by the ladies of ancient India? Adorned as if for her final dream, she seems to slump on the ground from the exhaustion of her own grandeur.

Meanwhile, in this courtyard of mortals, people get weaker by the day, like a crescent moon eroded by the powerful sapphire sky. Once they fall unconscious from their struggle to breathe in intensive care, do the patients feel they're floating in a beautiful dream? As they travel to the world of eternity, do they find the beauty in what we once overlooked? Do they recover what we've lost between the lines? Do they notice the pollen dusting a butterfly's wings, or catch the faint hum of its flutter? In death, perhaps, the divine in the details will reveal itself to us.

Dreaming, We Become Human

The rat is real, of this there can be no doubt; but Fulkumari, and the relationship I've built with her, are figments of my imagination. Isolated from the rest of the world, I'm confined to a mystifying space where my mind has been constructing her persona. It was with regret that Michel Foucault claimed the mysterious entities we call "I," "my will," "self," "soul," and so on don't really exist. They're just boxes, he said, into which the world bolts us to enforce the rule and discipline of the system, and what we consider a "mind" is really just a substance manufactured the same way as every other artificial product in the world. But here, in the solitude of lockdown, it's my mind that's creating Fulkumari. As the din of the outside world recedes, I feel that my mind is my own, and I am its master.

What we know as the real world—as it existed before being rudely interrupted by the pandemic—wasn't truly ruled by man, was it? The world, just as it existed, was the true master. People were driven by fear, greed, anxiety, hubris, the instinctive pleasures and pains of living, the pleasures and pains of the world. But it's only when humans come to see themselves beyond the worldliness of the world, when they begin to rise as subjects beyond the horizons of the world, that they cease to simply be living creatures and actually become human beings.

We may resemble other creatures, or even have needs that echo theirs. But although humans are part of nature, they're capable of seeing themselves apart from it. They can see themselves as "I." They can see others as "you." They can realise that they're independent beings with the power to think for themselves and change their conditions. This realisation, though, is never complete; it dawns on people individually, and continuously. We're always in the process of realising the "mind" that isn't subject to the world, and whose possibilities aren't limited to its confines.

Interlude

When people embark on this realisation, they become preoccupied with this "I," they try to create a world consistent with the one they have in their minds. And if they don't find that reflection of the mind in the real world, they begin to dream of a future with a different world. But people don't just ruminate on this new world; they fight to bring it about. They don't hesitate to sacrifice their lives in pursuit of this world, for the mere possibility of something that doesn't even exist. They aren't afraid to be martyred for the sake of a chapter of history that's yet to be written.

This isn't to say that the outcome of such a struggle needs to be good. Fascists, too, imagine a world and do everything in their might to bring it into existence. And the worlds we create in our minds, even with the best intentions, are static things, doomed to wither and rot once they're brought into existence if they don't know how to change and grow along with it. Perhaps our best revolutionaries are the failed ones, as they enable us to keep the dream alive for another day. For dream we must, and dreaming, we become human.

Humans make this discovery over and over again—as poets, as thinkers, as artists, as anything they can be. For many, this fight for change is akin to worship; these are the people whom we call "great." They realise that the way we see ourselves at present needn't be our last or only form, that it's only a particular form constructed in relation to the present world and its attachments. They're overcome by curiosity, wondering what exactly God created us for, or investigating why humans emerged in the first place. They engage in the task of rediscovering and reconstructing the meaning of their own existence. It is this task that makes us essentially human, and it is their engagement with this task that makes them great to us.

As civilisation appears to be retreating behind closed doors, human beings are retrieving the mystifying world within themselves. The lockdown has trapped us in our minds, giving us the opportunity to rediscover them. It has allowed our minds to regain their power and authority over themselves. The pandemic has bestowed on us a collective opening that a world devoid of it would never have offered.

The Hospital

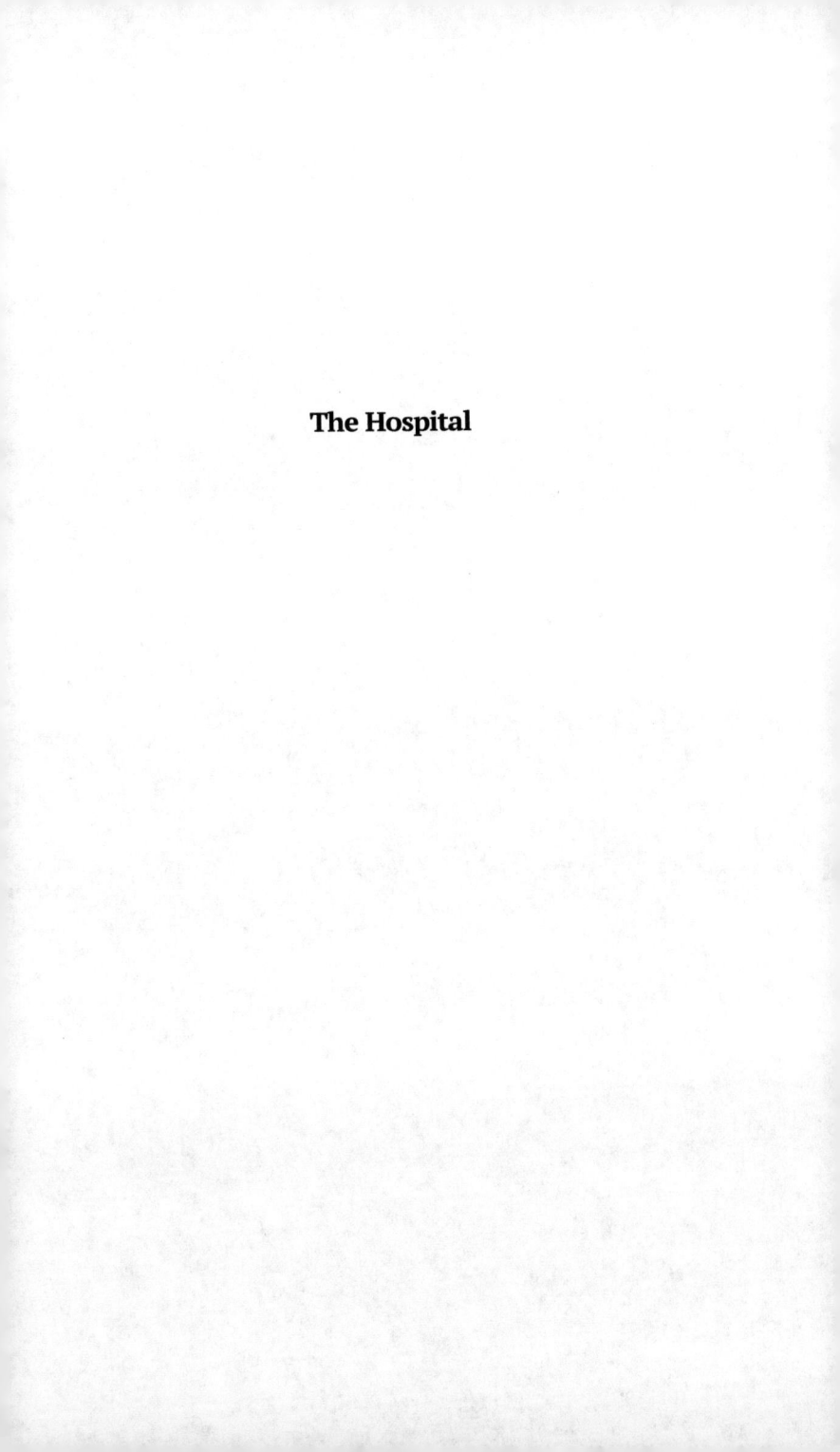

The Missed Farewell

A phone call from the doctor wakes me up in the morning. He's trying to help me regulate my heart rate. Lately, it has become so high that I can't bring it under control no matter what. I don't know why, but my heart always starts to race while I'm asleep. I'm startled awake every time, as if by a suffocating fish flailing about inside my rib cage. All day, I hope for the excruciating feeling to go away; all day, it racks me, and then, as suddenly as it came, it disappears. At night, I can't go to sleep without fear and anticipation gnawing at my mind. My entire body is ruined.

The doctor, who is my age, tells me he has faced the same problem and was cured by a procedure called ablation. The heartbeat consists of electrical impulses produced in a certain part of the heart. But in cases like ours, he says, there are other parts that start producing these impulses as well. It's almost like there's a second heart in my heart, beating to its own, erratic drum. He says he will find these parts, reach them with a probe, and burn them. The cells will die, my heart will scar, and my second heartbeat will cease.

The doctor gives me the exact date and time of my surgery and walks me through the preparation schedule. I'd assumed that during the pandemic, such elective procedures would be stopped. But no, the endless work of healing hasn't come to a halt.

I have to stay at the hospital for a few days. I'm leaving Fulkumari behind. I look for her everywhere, in vain. I wish I could have seen her one last time; it would have been only apt to take my leave from her formally. Please forgive me, I should have said, in case I don't return. Let go of the memory of this wrongdoing of mine. Should I never set foot in this house again, it will be under your care—until the next tenant arrives. But Fulkumari is nowhere to be found. I set off for the hospital with a different kind of anguish in my heart.

I have to take the metro, something I haven't done in a while. The station is lifeless and empty; I'm the only one on the platform. I sink into a seat and wait for one of the few running trains to arrive. Finally, it does, startling me with its sound. I enter and sit down, all by myself inside the eerie, vibrating carriage. The metro starts moving noisily, and I notice that it doesn't even make all the usual stops. It just keeps rolling from one empty station to the next, humming and droning incessantly. The subterranean world of machines appears unbothered, keeping up its routine even though the people have disappeared from the scene.

At the hospital, I'm greeted by the opposite sight. An endless number of ambulances are filing in, their petrifying sirens never falling silent. Nurses and paramedics, like astronauts in their PPE, are taking the patients off the vehicles and disappearing with them inside the building. Their faces are all concealed, but somehow I can sense their fear, frustration, and pain all the same.

Passing by the emergency ward, I make my way to my designated centre. There, I find everything already laid out and arranged for me. I keep my bag on the table and lay my body on the spotless white bed.

Indra's Blessing

I've fallen asleep, suffused with exhaustion and foreboding about the next day's operation. As if overwhelmed by the fragrance of Mandar Kusum, I'm visited by a dream. Going to bed with an anxious mind is supposed to bring on nightmares, but my dream is strangely beautiful. The dread and fear of death dissipate as I watch Indra, the king of gods, bestow me with an elixir of immortality. There's no terror anymore, no pandemic, no death; all I know here is a life of everlasting joy without tears. Youth doesn't wane, the body doesn't decay, and nothing gets tarnished. Saying goodbye is painless, separation without agony, and there are no sad sighs.

All of a sudden, my dream is cut short by another fragrance. I open my eyes to see a young doctor before me; the sweet smell comes from her hair. She tells me she'll supervise my tests. Before anything else, they need to collect a sample for a Covid test. Covid patients don't have access to the operating theatre; they're untouchables everywhere in the hospital except in their own ward.

"Touch me not," Jesus said to Mary Magdalene after his resurrection, exhorting her to touch others in the spirit of love. But although the Son of God lives on amongst the people as the universal spirit of love, intangible if not untouchable, mankind hasn't always benefited from it. Sometimes it's impossible to walk towards happiness or love. And sometimes, you just have to walk away from life. Leaves that have shrivelled in the drought yearn for the first drop of rain. The clouds also want to give them a shower. But sometimes, the time just isn't right. It doesn't rain. Hope, faith, and love, even when combined with myriad possibilities, aren't enough to make all buds blossom; they have to live with that eternal sorrow. One day, the sky above will be sweet, as will be the air. *Oh, deep in my heart, I know that I do believe... We shall overcome, someday.*

The nurse inserts a cotton swab stick in my nose. It goes deep into my nostril, and when it scrapes against my nasal wall, it feels like it has reached the crown of my head. The sharp pain casts a darkness over my vision. Next, the doctor sits down by the bed and conducts my echocardiogram. "There's some risk involved in the surgery, for sure," she says slowly, handing me a sheet of paper to take my written consent. "The phrenic nerve may get injured." What would happen then, I ask while mechanically signing the form. "It could cause some complications. You might not be able to breathe without support."

That would mean having to depend on a machine for the rest of my life. If God were to come before me and wish to bless me then, would I ask for death? Blessings are supposed to endow one's life with happiness and well-being. But the blessing of God could also free me from a life of torture. Our addiction to life is precisely what makes us unhappy. If you are without thirst, you won't be crestfallen if you can't have water.

A life without addiction must be a happy one, but I can't quite imagine what sort of happiness that would be. A fish doesn't desire the firmament because it's oblivious to the azure of the sky. There's no murmur of longing for the Amaranth in the soul of the forest bee, for it has never heard about it. The heart of the wild deer doesn't cry out for the ocean because the sound of the saline water has never entered its dream.

Like a child, I close my eyes and picture the scene: God has appeared before me as I'm held captive by the machine. My chest heaves like a frantically shaking hand. The instrument makes a humming sound. I cannot move. God begins to speak to me in a deep voice. "Prepare yourself to receive my blessing," he says. "Prepare to free yourself from attachment and addiction forever."

"Please," I reply, "let my death arrive upon your blessing. Let me fall into a deep, deep slumber. I will reunite with the truth."

The Hospital

The next morning, as they take me to the operation, I oscillate between consciousness and sleep. The operating rooms maintain a chilly environment under strict temperature control. As I recline on the surgical table, the coldness seeps in, making me tremble.

"Would you like to listen to music?" the doctor asks.

"Music? In French?"

"No," he says. "Any music you like. We can find it online."

"Could you play this one song for me—"Tomaro Ashime Prano Mono Loye"… by Tagore?"

The doctor nods, and in the blink of an eye, the room starts brimming with an indescribable beauty.

> With all my heart and soul, I race towards your infinite vastness.
> There is no more sadness, no more death, no separation anymore.
> The instant I turn away from you unto my puny self,
> Only then does death take on its form and suffering lay its trap.
>
> O Infinite, within your sacred abode
> Lies every dream and vision I behold.
>
> Selfishly deluding me that they belong to me,
> This callow self laments day and night.
>
> When you are at the centre of my life,
> All my self-pity, all the weight of this world
> Vanishes in the blink of an eye.

Putting the anesthesia mask over my face, the doctor asks me to breathe. I know that in a flash, I will be lulled into a deep sleep. Before taking that final breath, I listen closely one more time. The words of the song seem to be floating in from afar—*There is no more sadness, no more death, no separation anymore.*

Music Is Life

The Covid unit is located just below my ward, and in the two days I spend in hospital after my procedure, I watch from my window as a steady, never-ending flow of patients arrives for treatment. But who makes it back home and who doesn't—that's impossible for me to tell. Scrolling through social media, I get the same feeling about Bangladesh; everybody's falling sick, but I can't determine the names that have popped up in the lottery of death. It's almost as if we're all dead and alive at the same time; like Schrödinger's cat, we won't know until someone checks.

In the fourteenth century, Europe was devastated by the Black Death. Men and women used to sing songs of death in churches and pubs; songs would stream out of the caves where the diseased were banished. Some even said they would prefer for the plague to never end; how else could they keep listening to the matchless music of death? In spite of my closeness to the Covid ward, I haven't heard any such music here.

The Black Death triggered the rebirth of Europe, and it lives on in many guises—like the *danse macabre*, a form of art portraying the dance of death. These images would be etched on the walls of homes and churches. In the final scene of Bergman's famous *Seventh Seal*, the angel of death dances as he leads the cast away.

Time and again, poets and artists have fallen in love with suffering, disease, and death. "O death," wrote Tagore, "I adore you like my beloved Shyam." In Hindu mythology, Shyam—Krishna, the black—is not just a god but also a lover. Tagore may have adored death as much as any European poet, but Bengal never got an actual Renaissance. Looking at the world around me now, I cannot really say whether this was a blessing or a curse.

There's a popular tale in my country, of an old woman who lived all by herself. If she died, her neighbours stood to take over her house and property, so they hurled bricks at her tin roof in the dead of the night to hasten her demise. The old woman couldn't sleep a wink after the sun went down. She sat by a burning candle, all alone, beating a bronze plate like a drum and singing along to the beat. She'd told the few good people to keep listening for her—should the playing stop, they would know that she had died.

Music is life, and its end is death. When a child is born in my country, Hindus intone the *Ulu-Dhwani*, while Muslims recite the *Azaan*—the call to prayer. We enter the mortal world with this music in our ears, and once we're gone, it's with music that our loved ones summon our memories. If the life we lead in between is tuneless, can we truly claim to have lived?

The Second Heart Unbent

It's time for me to leave the hospital. They hand me a discharge letter, and the nurse asks if I need a taxi—the fare, she says, is covered by social security. I nod, she leaves to make the call, and I begin to pack my bag. Just then, all of a sudden, my heart starts pounding again. I ring for the nurse, but by the time she arrives, it has calmed down. She chuckles, saying it was a false alarm and I was worried for nothing. I tell her I'm a doctor and I know atrial fibrillation when I feel it. She just shakes her head and leaves. As soon as she's out of sight, the pounding starts again. This time, I walk over to the nurse station myself. "Here," I say, "feel my pulse." They check properly and raise their eyebrows.

"You walked all the way here? In this state?"

"What was I supposed to do? You didn't believe me when I told you it was atrial fibrillation."

"Quick, lie down on the stretcher!"

"That won't be necessary," I say, heading back. "I can walk to the room on my own."

A few minutes later, I hear all of them rushing down the aisle towards my room. They arrive equipped with ECG, echo, the works, but all these arrangements don't seem to bother my second heart, which is back to flip-flopping inside my chest like a fish out of water. They give me some pills and tell me I should try to get some sleep. But despite the sedatives, my heart is so agitated that I toss and turn, unable to tell if I'm truly sleeping or not.

Luckily, a few hours later, the fibrillation truly bids me farewell. The doctor informs me that this may continue for a couple more days. They haven't been able to stop my second heart for good. Should the trouble resume, they'll have to perform the whole procedure again.

"Should I call the taxi now?" the nurse asks.

"Perhaps I should stay here for today? I'm worried it will start again."

"We can't keep you any longer, unfortunately. You've been officially released from the system, so we have no choice but to let you go. Hopefully, the problem won't arise again. But if it does, just come back to the emergency ward. So, should I call the taxi?"

"Sure," I say dejectedly. After all, the system doesn't exist for our sake. To the contrary, we only exist as long as we're in the system. I suppose Plato was right. We're all tied up in the cave, looking at mere reflections, taking them for reality, and basing our actions on them. And even if someone tries to show us the truth, our topsy-turvy logic is so dear to us that we cannot give it up.

Melody of Trees

In the taxi, it occurs to me that this is my first time taking a car since the lockdown began. I notice something new: a plastic sheet that divides the passenger from the driver. I'm reminded of excessively wealthy or important people who never see the face of the person driving them around. Perhaps they feel uncomfortable at the thought of another human being, made of flesh and blood, holding their lives in their hands as they wield the steering wheel. At least, I can still see my driver and even talk to him. But the pandemic has unfurled a transparent veil of estrangement between us.

After a short drive down the lifeless streets of Paris, I catch sight of the horse chestnut tree that tells me I'm home. I've developed a habit of talking to this tree whenever I pass by—silently, of course, in case there's someone around. As I try in vain to engage the tree in conversation, I sometimes guess at its age—I can measure the age of trees in Bangladesh just by looking at them, but those in France are new and strange to me.

It takes decades for a tree to form its rings. Slowly but surely, it grows a thick and darkened bark while nourishing the precious gilded matter inside. Its rings bear witness to everything—floods, draughts, human vanity—gathering an immense knowledge that the tree humbly chooses not to exercise. We can only learn what it knows if we cut it open and examine its rings. I read somewhere that if you play the rings of a tree like a record, they produce a melody. When the doctors cut me open on the operating table, did they hear my song as well?

The familiar scent of my apartment welcomes me as I open the door. Slowly, my eyes take in everything, finding it exactly as I left. In fact, even the food that I'd left behind for Fulkumari is still in the same spot, untouched. I settle into my chair and silently wait for her to show up.

The Hospital

After the civil war, when we were about to leave India and go back home, Baba bought me a miniature motorcycle. It had a rider, too, and he could be taken off and refitted as I liked. I carefully placed the gift inside a pocket in Ma's trunk for safekeeping. But when I came back a few days later, it wasn't there. A couple more days went by, and I returned to look for my toy in the same spot again. It still wasn't there. I kept coming back and searching for it, waiting a few days each time before resuming my hunt. But the motorcycle never reappeared. It was gone forever.

While at the hospital, the thought of Fulkumari never left my mind. Was she still at home? Was she eating properly? What if she thought I'd abandoned her? Had she pardoned me for not saying goodbye? Or did she now consider me no better than all the others who stole the land that was hers for millions of years, only to cover it in concrete? I get up and scan the familiar spots—the corner where I served her meals, the left side of my armchair where she used to sit and listen to me. But she's nowhere to be found. Just like Baba's motorcycle, she's gone—perhaps forever.

Suddenly, I'm struck by the realisation that this is not my home. I'm stranded in a dusty, soulless desert. Fulkumari, who once seemed so close, is just a distant mirage. I lean back into my armchair, motionless as the final rays of the sun take their leave. Soon, the harsh light of the night sky penetrates my chest, seeping into my heart. Somewhere between the moonlight and the shadows is Fulkumari, immersed in that mysterious, dreamlike world.

After Fulkumari

Kojagari Night

Mysteriously, the second lockdown in Paris starts on an auspicious date. It's Kojagari Night, when we venerate the divine lovers of Hindu mythology, such as Radha and Krishna, Shiva and Parvati, Lakshmi and Narayana, along with Chandra, the goddess of the moon. I wish Fulkumari were here to join me as I embark on this act of reverence, and the thought of being isolated again, but this time without her companionship, fills me with anxiety. She hasn't shown her face once in the months that have passed since I came back from the hospital.

Turning off the nightlight, I try to picture the flood of moonlight that must be washing over Bengal in all its brilliance tonight. Under the Kojagari full moon, fairies come down to the lakes from the sky, playing in the waters. In the evenings that follow, myriad beetles and flies, tiny and large, crowd into our house. For us children, this is a message: it's time to get ready for Deepavali, the Festival of Lights. Slowly, the moon erodes, feeling the pull of Amanisha—the night of the new moon. What an incredible night of complete darkness it is, the pure light of the moon swallowed in a sea of quiescence and silent meditation!

The ancient cultures of India have left us with layer upon layer of feasts and celebrations. Deepavali is directly preceded by Bhoot Chaturdashi—the Fourteenth of the Ghosts, the Bengali Day of the Dead. This is the day when our ancestors, spanning fourteen generations, come down to visit their descendants. To welcome their spirits, we light fourteen earthen lamps, their flickering flames casting gentle shadows and illuminating dark corners. The air grows thick with the scent of burning wood and the faint aroma of lamps. To appease the spirits, we prepare and eat fourteen different types of greens. Children like myself scour gardens and fields to gather them. We present our discoveries and explain their significance, accompanied by the rustling of leaves, the laughter of peers, and the approving nods of elders.

We close the day by burning effigies of another kind of spirit, haunting the earth with malicious intent, under the dark night sky. The spirits' skulls, crafted from earthen pots and placed atop straw, makeshift bodies, crackle as the flames take hold. The shattering of the skulls with the resonant thwack of a stick, a privilege reserved for the makers of the effigies, marks the release of the spirits into the night.

Then comes Deepavali, where the harsh breaking of skulls yields to a night of gentle observance. Hindus get busy with preparations even before the evening sets in—exchanging greetings, taking blessings from elders and giving blessings to younger ones, paying homage to Jamraj, the god of death, lighting the lamps once again to show their ancestors the way home, setting lamps afloat on banana leaves in the water, and praying for their ancestors before lights glowing in their honour. Houses, rooms, rooftops, gardens, courtyards are all decked out in lights. Of course, there's an endless, delicious supply of *luchi*, *labra*, and *payesh*.

At the Festival of Lights, quite like the Greek feast of Apollo, the murk of ignorance gives way to pure illumination. Pour light into these eyes, O Lord! The burning lamp surrenders itself in an act of faith, embellishing the sable empyrean of Amanisha with a dot of pristine light on her forehead. The Saptarshi Mandal shines like a group of diamonds floating in the sky. Minutes roll by, and the night grows more enigmatic. The darkness awakens a longing for infinity. It is as if the world of our feelings is merely an illusion of superficial beauty. As the moon prepares to end her Amanisha meditation and return in her new form, we go from peaceful to restless.

In the wake of Kojagari, the night jasmines become more fragrant than ever before. Paris is famous for its alluring scents, and I know there's a metro station that bears the name of Jasmin.

After Fulkumari

If I were to visit it, would it welcome me with the long-lost fragrance of those Bengali night jasmines? Your sense of smell is wasted if you've never inhaled their scent in the morning. Alas, I'm confined to this apartment once again. Perhaps, from tomorrow, beetles and flies will visit me here as well?

But it isn't just the jasmine or the flying, crawling evening callers—all of nature is in tune with Kojagari. The catkins take their leave, saying, "I'll be back next year. Take care, all of you." The rivers and canals of Bengal grow more serene, and the water lilies on the Padma are matchless in their enchantment. The fragrance of love is harboured in their pollen. The wind plays the song of autumn in the paddy fields. The green of the mango, jackfruit, and black plum trees deepens in the twilight.

Suddenly, it begins to rain. The moonlight melts into droplets of water before making its way down to the earth. Then, on the stroke of midnight, that one thing happens again, just as it did outside our Bogra house, by the Altafunnesa playground. Softly, haltingly, it calls to me. Is it just my imagination? Who would call through this heavy rain in such a broken voice? It's a kitten, completely drenched, crying outside my window. But the moment I open the door, it runs away. Until now, it was calling for me; now I'm the one who's calling. My voice gets drowned in the sound of the rain; I can't see through the dark. The rain isn't bothered. It just continues to fall.

Jesus of Palestine

As the year draws to a close, Covid cases go down a little, and lockdown restrictions are relaxed. As long as you wear a mask, you can go out whenever you want, and even order a meal at a restaurant, although you'll still have to eat it outside. The experts tell us, however, that we're only past the first wave; like in a tsunami, it'll be followed by another, quite likely stronger than its predecessor.

My graduate courses, which I'd been taking online, have shifted back to the university. I can finally see my classmates again, even go out with them, and visit the few friends I have in Paris. But things are not the same: I fear coming close to people, and I dread physical contact. Any sudden, unexpected touch makes me feel like I need to rush home and take a shower, and I don't even want to shake hands anymore. As the physical barriers between us are lifted, I seem to seek an invisible barrier instead. And I observe a similar attitude in others: on more than one occasion, people move away from me when I sit down next to them in the lecture hall.

On the street, as I breathe out into my mask, my glasses get fogged up. But as annoying as it is to have my vision go blurry like that, seeing everything around me clear up again does give me a sense of hope.

In the meantime, Christmas approaches, waiting for nothing and no one—not even the plague itself. Back in my country, one cannot even tell when it's Christmas—there's no weather to indicate it and no decoration to match, except for the occasional fake pine tree put up by some five-star hotel for the benefit of its Western guests. But in Europe, Christmas arrives like a swift-footed steed, like the grand processions accompanying the major festivals in Bangladesh.

When I was a child, missionaries used to visit our playgrounds and schools. The locals didn't mind them; Christianity, after all, is an Abrahamic religion just like Islam, and conversion from one to the other hadn't become a debated issue yet. The different communities respected each other's religion, and, in fact, shared in each other's sense of holiness. At the big market of Bogra, there was a shrine for Muslims and a temple for Hindus, and whenever we visited the temple, we made an offering at the shrine as well.

The missionaries would give us beautifully bound bibles, along with pre-paid postcards that had some questions on them which you could answer if you read certain chapters. If you sent the right answers back, you'd receive some gifts, like pencils, pens, erasers, and other postcards with nice views. You'd also get more postcards with questions that you could answer for more gifts. I played this game for a while before tiring of it.

One such day, I was reading the Gospel of Matthew. It opens with the events of Jesus' birth:

> Now the birth of Jesus Christ was on this wise: when as his mother Mary was espoused to Joseph, before they came together, she was found with child of the Holy Ghost. Then Joseph her husband, being a just man, and not willing to make her a public example, was minded to put her away privily. But while he thought on these things, behold, the angel of the Lord appeared unto him in a dream, saying, Joseph, thou son of David, fear not to take unto thee Mary thy wife: Ffor that which is conceived in her is of the Holy Ghost. And she shall bring forth a son, and thou shalt call his name Jesus: for he shall save his people from their sins.

A question arose in the child's mind—so, didn't Jesus have a father? I asked Baba about it.

Baba was still for a while. "He was born from the Holy Spirit," he finally said, "on God's orders. He was holy."

The answer wasn't exactly satisfying, so I dug deeper into the text.

> Now when Jesus was born in Bethlehem of Judaea in the days of Herod the king, behold, there came wise men from the east to Jerusalem, saying, Where is he that is born King of the Jews? For we have seen his star in the east, and are come to worship him.

I closed my eyes, trying to imagine the three wise men walking under the night sky, looking for Jesus.

> And, lo, the star, which they saw in the east, went before them, till it came and stood over where the young child was. When they saw the star, they rejoiced with exceeding great joy.

There was a picture of Jesus hanging in our living room, along with a big photo of Lenin and a drawing of Mother Kali. It showed the Baby Jesus in the arms of the guiltless Mary, surrounded by a couple of lambs chewing on their cud. It was an image from an old calendar, the kind they used to give as gifts at supermarkets, and it was slightly torn at one of its upper corners. Even a feeble blow of wind was enough to make it flutter. And yet, the compassionate eyes of the young mother Mary never changed, as if eternally new.

No matter his paternity, Jesus was a Palestinian by blood, with brown skin and the heart of a communist. He was a refugee all his life, and still is one today, his very identity stolen by those who render him with fair skin and blue eyes. Today, the three wise men could never have crossed the wall and barbed wire to reach him in Bethlehem. Or maybe, today, the star would have led them elsewhere, to the dwelling of a Rohingya mother, for instance, whom Pope Francis so generously decreed to be no less an image of the living God. When I think of the Rohingya, I'm stunned by the realisation that I live in a world where even refugee status can be a luxury.

Humiliating Scrutiny

Winter in Paris stands in stark contrast to my homeland, where the need for heavy clothing is a rarity. My weekday classes are all in the afternoons, and coming home late in the biting cold is a challenge. To make matters worse, Paris is experiencing an unusual snowfall this year. At a metro station, a billboard catches my eye: a warm, red jacket on sale. Enticed, I go to the store and buy one. It proves a saviour against the harsh weather, and it has large pockets and compartments, spacious enough to carry small books. When I wear it, I don't even need to carry a bag, and being tall, I don't mind its bulging pockets.

My Paris shopping routine includes a thrifty habit, nurtured during my early days of hardship here—a regular hunt for nearly expired food items on sale. The supermarket near my apartment is a frequent haunt for me, its shelves lined with an abundance of perishable products. Yet the store's image is marred by its ever-present, unsmiling guards, whose stern faces and irritable demeanour cast a shadow over the aisles.

One day, as I stand at the checkout, I witness a scene that captures the essence of misguided fear and suspicion. A young Arab boy, no older than ten, a bottle of milk clutched in his small, trembling hands, is roughly seized by a guard. As he's marched back to the counter, the boy's face drains of colour. The cashier examines the milk before returning it with a gentle confirmation of its purchase. I exhale a breath I didn't know I was holding, relieved and disturbed in equal measure. I think of Victor Hugo—has the boy actually committed the theft, only to be silently pardoned by a compassionate soul?

I don't imagine, at this moment, that I will soon find myself in the boy's shoes. Leaving the supermarket empty-handed on a day when my hunt yields no near-expired treasures, I'm abruptly halted by the same guard. His suspicion-laden gaze zeroes in on the bulges of my jacket. He slides his hands in my pockets as if I don't deserve any personal boundaries. The humiliation is palpable as I produce the innocent contents of my jacket one by one: some small books, a coin pouch, my mobile charger, a power bank, my old e-reader carrying echoes of Bangladesh, a notebook, a handkerchief, a few pens, and my spectacle case. The guard's frustration at his fruitless search mounts with each item, yet he offers no apology.

The reality of being perceived as the other hits me with jarring force. My modest attire and the colour of my skin, coupled with a demeanour that perhaps speaks of my foreign roots, has singled me out in the guard's eyes. He seems to have marked me, not just as an outsider, but as someone who doesn't belong to his world, doesn't fit in the fabric of his society.

At that moment, as I stand there, feeling the mortifying sting of his scrutiny, I think of Fulkumari and how such judgements had no place in our shared existence. "O blessed one," I find myself musing, "in all our time together, you neither had to justify your presence nor put up with any misplaced mistrust. And yet, sometimes you didn't even accept the offerings I brought you. And yet, in the end, you left me all alone."

Much later, after both hardship and confinement have ended, I'll find myself honouring this spirit of offering. Guards will still be everywhere—unyielding, unfeeling, they'll stand like silent sentinels at the gates of the glass-and-steel fortress that I'll come to call my workplace. Is it the monotony of their duty—the ceaseless parade of employees, visitors, and delivery personnel—that has chiselled away their humanity? Or maybe it is us, the people passing through, with our hurried footsteps and distracted glances, that turn them into a mere part of the structure, that etch the same stern expression onto all their faces?

One day, as I shuffle towards the coffee counter, I'll notice something unexpected: a jar of small, square chocolates nestled among the muffins and biscotti. I'll pick up a few, and the same evening, while leaving the office, I'll approach the guards, extending my hand, the foil-wrapped treats inside. They'll eye me with suspicion, their gazes shifting from my hand to my face, as if unsure whether to accept or rebuff this unexpected peace offering. In the end, they'll take the chocolates. And something will shift.

Day by day, I'll repeat the ritual. As I approach, they'll no longer stand rigidly at attention, leaning against the glass doors instead, their eyes crinkling with familiarity. We'll chat briefly about the weather, the news, or their family weekends. We'll exchange smiles—a currency more valuable than any paycheck.

Flames Engulf the Landscape

Apart from its windows onto the street, my apartment has two other windows onto the world: the screens of my laptop and my phone. Ever since Fulkumari vanished, I've spent most of my time indoors looking out through one of them. This isn't new to me: even before the pandemic, and even before my exile, these two screens were my preferred means of reaching out to the world. Often, I feel lonely in crowds, and the time I spend with most people isn't necessarily chosen, let alone enjoyable. So much better to filter your exposure to the world through a screen. The only problem now, as Paris enters its third round of confinement, is that this lifestyle is no longer a choice but an imposition.

Today, social media echoes with the sounds of war. The clash at the Al-Aqsa mosque in Jerusalem has sparked a fierce battle in the Gaza Strip between Hamas and the Israeli forces. Equipped with the most advanced arms, Israel is bombing the Strip without mercy. As if in a movie, the inhabitants of a Gazan building receive a phone call from the Israeli army, telling them to evacuate. Less than an hour later, the building is razed to the ground by a remote controlled missile. In response, Hamas launches a homemade rocket at Israel. Not that it causes much harm—in most cases, the Israeli army manages to neutralise it long before it reaches the ground. It's a ruthless, oppressive war, with one side so much more powerful than the other, and with countless women, children, and elderly losing their lives.

The kings and rulers of the past were also tyrannical, ruthless, oppressive, belligerent. There has never been an emperor who didn't fight at least one battle in his lifetime, including the only two rulers in India's five-thousand-year history who could be called truly great: Ashoka and Jalal-ud-din Akbar. While these two may have gone to war, they came back with an ache in their hearts after witnessing their subjects' plight. Akbar was affectionately called Dillishwaro Jagadishwaro Ba—God of Delhi and God of the World. Even though he was a Muslim, he was revered like a deity among Hindus.

Ashoka, for his part, was called Devanampiya Piyadassi—Beloved of the Gods, and He Who Regards With Kindness. He only fought one war in his lifetime, the Kalinga War, and it cost the lives of one hundred thousand soldiers in a single battle. Late at night, once the fighting was done, Ashoka went to inspect the battlefield. The gruesome sight of the corpses sent a chill down his spine. In the distant darkness, he saw a flickering light and ordered his men to bring him the person bearing it. It was a Buddhist ascetic, a shraman. Ashoka asked him what he was doing there, on the battlefield, amidst the sea of corpses, in the middle of the night.

"Your Majesty," the shraman replied courteously, "as you have served death, I am serving life."

"What do you mean?" Ashoka asked.

"There are some soldiers on the battlefield who are still alive, whimpering in pain," the shraman said. "I'm giving them water to drink."

Ashoka was overwhelmed. Ordering his soldiers to rescue all who were still alive, he took the shraman to his palace. The shraman told him all about the Buddha's teachings, and Ashoka listened. Soon, he converted to Buddhism, and vowed to never set foot on a battlefield again.

Indeed, he stayed true to his word. His empire grew enormous—the largest to ever exist in India, spanning from Bengal to Afghanistan to Persia—but he never had to fight to conquer any land. Awed by his benevolence and generosity, the other rulers gave it to him willingly.

One photograph from Palestine keeps haunting my screen and my thoughts—a man, a smile on his face, is performing the last rites for his wife and his son, both killed in a bombing. I'm a husband and father myself, and for the life of me, I can't fathom how I could manage to muster a smile after losing the two people dearest to me.

I think of another man who suffered the same loss—Joe Biden, the US politician, whose wife and daughter were killed in an accident. What's the difference between him and the Palestinian father? Maybe it's that Biden is forever denied meaning in the randomness of his loss. Maybe it's that the Palestinian father can give meaning even to his pain, a meaning that lets him stand tall, with a smile on his face, even at his loved ones' funeral. The Buddha said that life is nothing but suffering and pain. If so, then suffering is where meaning must be found.

I had an uncle, Rabi, whom I used to call Ranga Kaku—Red Uncle. He doted on me; in fact, he loved me so much that he even tried to talk my parents into letting him adopt me. Like my uncle Boro Jethu, who was twenty-two years his senior, Ranga Kaku was an activist. He'd taken the common path from the Student Union to the Communist Party and spent the civil war fundraising and organising refugees in India. Once the war was over, he'd become the founding editor of Bogra's first daily newspaper.

Ranga Kaku was usually at the editorial office when we paid family visits to his home, so we'd call him up on the phone. I spent entire visits like that, with the phone glued to my ear, in the hope of hearing his mechanical voice. With his curly hair and guileless smile, he looked just like the Bangladeshi film star Rajjak.

From writing to football to singing, it seemed there was nothing Ranga Kaku wasn't good at. Baba used to say that if he put all his time into writing, he'd be as famous as Kamal Kumar Majumdar, and if he focused on music instead, he'd be no less known than Bob Dylan. When the Bogra Youth Choir started out as the cultural front of the Communist Party, Ranga Kaku was behind the scenes. He wrote their lyrics and composed their melodies. The song I liked the best was called "Flames Engulf the Landscape." The beginning was sung in a single voice:

> Flames engulf the landscape, FLAMES!
> In Hanoi, in Haifa,
> Through Hiroshima's heart, flames rage on,
> Turning verdant expanses
> Into mere whispers of ash.

Following this, everyone sang the chorus in unison:

> Flames engulf the landscape! FLAMES!

When you listened to it, it felt as if the sound was piercing your heart.

But Ranga Kaku never got the chance to be a Kamal Kumar Majumdar or Bob Dylan. Instead, like me, he was given the gift of exile. In 1974, when Sheikh Mujib turned Bangladesh into a one-party state with the support of the Communist Party, my uncle became a prominent state official. But just over a year later, a military coup ended the oppressive regime, Sheikh Mujib and his family were executed, and many party members were arrested or killed. Ranga Kaku's home was hit by a bomb, and he fled with his wife and daughter to Siliguri, a small city across the Indian border, where he lived out the rest of his life teaching at a local high school.

Many decades later, in 2009, I managed to lure him on a trip back to his home country. I put him up at a hotel close to my office, in the heavily fortified Dhanmondi precinct of Dhaka. The hotel was right next door to the headquarters of BDR, the Bangladeshi border security force, and as fate would have it, the morning after Ranga Kaku checked in, a mutiny broke out and dozens of people were killed. My mortified uncle left the same day, never to return.

Fulkumari

"Poetry," Miroslav Holub once said, "emerges when all else has failed, when chaos becomes unbearable and the last vestige of order must be restored. Poets rise in times of dire need—when freedom, vitamin C, communication, laws, and remedies for hypertension are scarce. To be a poet is to embrace failure, for art is born from the loyalty to what falls apart." It's in this spirit that I remember my uncle's songs. Revolution was out of reach for him and his comrades; and yet, they penned verses, ever the loyal companions of failure, finding strength and solace in the rhythm of their words.

A Nation of Refugees

I'm not giving up hope of seeing my dear Fulkumari again. And even though she hasn't yet granted me the privilege of her company during this third confinement, sometimes I still speak to her, talking out loud so that she'll know I haven't forgotten her or our shared promise.

Today, I want to tell Fulkumari that being a refugee isn't my fault. It's a destiny embedded in the journey our people embarked upon thousands of years ago. We are, in fact, a nation of refugees, no matter how much we may deny it, trying to cover up the trauma of our splintered faiths and lands. We carry the golden sunsets of our lost homeland in our hearts, just as the melodies of ancient songs and the echoes of our lost seven rivers ring in our ears.

Europe doesn't know rivers that make exiles of people in their own land. Its rivers are calm; they've been following the same course for thousands of years. The flooding of the river Seine in 1910 is remembered even today; in Bangladesh, it wouldn't even warrant a footnote in history. Our rivers are like volcanoes; thousands of them flow all across the nation, and their silt is what forms the country's land. They change their faces with every new year, with every new season, swamping and wreaking havoc on homesteads, dwellings, memories, everything, and causing the people to flee. But just as they destroy one bank, the rivers create another one, bringing forth an abundant supply of fertile soil. In no time, the surrounding land gets enveloped in a blanket of lush green plants and crops. Life starts anew.

Even though many civilisations have sunk deep beneath the currents, never to surface again, we still remember our people's most ancient culture, forged in the valley of yet another great river—the Indus. In fact, the Indus Valley was made up of seven rivers, so mighty that the people on their banks held them in the same esteem as the sea, calling them Sapta Sindhu—the Seven Seas. Flowing out of the Hindu Kush and the Himalayas, the Sapta Sindhu made their way through Kashmir, blended into the Indus around Punjab, and travelled through Sindh before reaching the ocean.

By all accounts, it was an age of prosperity and abundance, with cities boasting systems of water supply, sewage, and streets that wouldn't look out of place today, and farms sustained by an intricate network of irrigation that could take water wherever it was needed. But one day, this civilisation was destroyed, bludgeoned by a cascade of innumerable floods. It seems that the catastrophe was caused by the people themselves, who built dam after dam, changing the course of the rivers and provoking their ire in unpredictable ways. Clearly, five thousand years ago, nature was as cruel and merciless in her revenge as she is today.

People used to imagine the land beyond the Seven Seas as a different world altogether, and even though we've long since traversed them today, they still guard the borders of our imagination. "I saw you on the other side of the Seven Seas," Shahanaz Rahmatullah and Abdul Jabbar sing, "and drew your image with the wings of the bees in my heart." The song opens with a mandolin part that makes one's heart flutter just like those bees.

I loved the tune so much that I learned to play it on the mandolin and practised it each morning during my years in Dhaka, hoping that it would envelop the rest of my day in its happiness. On most days, it didn't work. The pharmaceutical industry I joined after deciding against a career as a doctor exposed me to corruption at all levels, from the medical profession to my team itself, and I ended most of my days in frustration and despair. Still, the next day, I made sure not to leave the house before playing the mandolin again, hoping that something would change. And on some occasions, it did seem to work. These were the moments when, just like our ancestors, I caught a glimpse of the other shore of the Seven Seas.

Rendered refugees, the Indus Valley people migrated to the banks of the river Saraswati, starting what is known as the Vedic Age. To them, the vast and swift Saraswati was more than just a river—she was a goddess. With their heads bowed, they offered her all the gratitude and reverence in their hearts. But then, one day, Saraswati was no more. The gushing water dried up, and the river disappeared, together with the swift-footed goddess herself. And once again, the journey of the refugees began, the blazing images of not one, but two lost civilisations seared beneath their eyelids. They conceived a proverb: the sea dries up wherever the ill-fated goes.

No less than half the people left the land, only to end up by another river, the Ganges, just as mighty as Saraswati, and, like her, descended from the heavens. Her story begins with King Bhagirathi, whose ancestors were reduced to ashes by the curse of a sage, Kapil Muni. In repentance for their transgressions, he went to the Himalayas to meditate, and in time, his spirit became as pure as the snow capping the mountains that surrounded him as far as his eyes could see. Satisfied with his worship, Brahma descended from the heavens. "Your austerity has pleased me," said the god, "ask of me what you wish."

Bhagirathi knew there was only one way that his ancestors could be released from the shackles of the curse. If the goddess Ganga were to descend from the firmament, his forefathers could use her holy water to purify themselves of their sins, emerging from hell to rejoin the cycle of reincarnation. Brahma granted Bhagirathi's wish, and in the holy water of Ganga, his forefathers found repentance.

As Ganga descended from the heavens, she received the blessing of Brahma, who told her that her sacrifice was for the good of humankind. "Your holy touch will not only cleanse the ancestors of Bhagirathi," he told her, "but the rest of humanity as well. You will be Patit Pawani, the One Who Purifies Sinners."

But Ganga was despondent. "The dwellers of the earth have sinned so much," she lamented. "They live in corruption and injustice, tell lies, and their hearts brim with hatred and greed—so much so that the earth itself is heavy with their sins. How can I carry such an enormous load on my waves?"

Brahma reassured her. "True," he said, "There are unjust and corrupt people in the world. But there are also many who are virtuous, whose bodies and minds brim with holiness. I reside within those pious souls. Their touch will rid your water of all the impurities that others might impart upon you."

In the thousands of years that have passed since then, the Ganges has washed off the sins of millions of people. But Brahma's words didn't prove to be true. The touch of the virtuous souls failed to free her from the sinners' burden. Today, the Ganges is the most polluted river in India. This is how she arrives in Bangladesh, where we call her Padma. And today, our ancestors' fate is playing itself out once again. Padma is drying up, along with so many of our rivers, just as Saraswati did before. Our people have taken to damming their flows, just as they did in the Indus Valley. Having lived as one for thousands of years, they're divided by borders now, and they're cutting off the rivers to dry each other into submission.

So this is why, Fulkumari, my absent friend, the fate of a refugee doesn't unnerve me. It's a fate that unites me with my homeland's past and present, that makes me one with my ancestors and my people, even when we're apart.

Bhusuku Is a Bengali

Another day begins in confinement without Fulkumari. She was an early riser, and her morning routine made me want to join her. In her absence, I sleep in late, and when I wake up, the silence is palpable. Once again, I decide to fill it with a story for her, clinging to the hope that she's still nearby, playing hide and seek, and will suddenly appear to my surprise.

"Fulkumari," I ask, "have you noticed that people seem to be much more confined by their fear than by the four walls that surround them? More than a year has passed, and still, the pandemic is all they ever seem to talk about."

In the East, pandemics are part of life: smallpox, malaria, kala-azar, tuberculosis—the list goes on. Cholera outbreaks have left thousands of villages deserted, with people abandoning their own relatives to their fate. In medical school, we were taken on field trips to witness the diseases of the community firsthand. But after coming back and opening our textbooks, all imported from the West, we found little to no trace of what we'd just seen. Our reality was as missing from those books as treatments are for our common diseases. Western pharmaceutical companies spend billions on hair loss, yet care little for plagues in other parts of the world.

This disregard is nothing new. When Hitler occupied much of Europe, he was merely mirroring centuries of European practice in Africa, America, Asia, and Australia. His fatal error was to bring colonisation and extermination to his neighbours rather than keeping it neatly out of sight. Without him and the havoc he wrought back at home, many of the world's colonies might have remained exactly that—colonies—to this day. Living under British rule when Britain itself was under threat, our people were shipped to Europe to fight and die. They were never asked if they wished to save their colonial masters from fascist invaders, nor were they asked if they saw much difference between the two.

Fulkumari

But the sorrow, the deep emotion that lies at the root of being Bengali didn't begin with these late-coming invaders from the West. Sorrow, I fear, is nothing less than our unifying glue, the common language that connects us to each other and our ancestors alike. It's in our songs, our poems, our oldest recorded texts. The word "Bengali" was first written down in the *Charyapada*, the oldest Bengali literary work. "Today, Bhusuku is a Bengali," writes Siddhacharya Bhusukupada, one of the *Charyapada*'s authors, "his wife taken by the Chandala..." A boatman on the Padma, he has lost everything to looting brigands, including his wife's dignity. It's in losing everything that he has become a Bengali, and it's this oppression and loss, rather than any kind of ethnicity, that has come to define his identity.

In our younger history, right before the British, there were the Marathas, visiting death and destruction upon Bengal on yearly raids from their kingdom that spanned most of India, just as Magh and Portuguese pirates raided the coasts of Bengal, capturing and enslaving the people who went on to become today's Rohingyas. And once again, history was kept alive in the poems and songs of the common people. "The baby is asleep," tells a popular lullaby, sung by every Bengali mother to this day, "the neighbourhood is quiet, the Marathas have come to the land. The *bulbul* birds have eaten the rice, how will we pay the tax?"

Other poems were less mindful of the sensitive ears of children. Here is how Gangaram, a Hindu poet from Bengal, described the wrath of the Maratha mercenaries, Hindus themselves:

> Everyone fled at the news of the Borgis' arrival. They wreaked havoc in the fields, looted gold and silver, and spared nothing in their paths. They cut off hands, noses, ears, or killed in a single stroke. They tied up the women and took turns in raping them, one finishing as the next began, heedless of their unbearable screams. The sky and the air wept, and even the stones called out to Krishna, Kali, Allah, and Bhagwan.

After Fulkumari

These poems, these songs come down to us in our common language, a language that unites all of us, from dozing baby to dying elder, from a peasant toiling in a paddy field to a scholar travelling the world. When the great Bengali Buddhist sage Atish Dipankar stepped into Tibet, a land that still practises the religion he introduced, a sight transported him back to his origins in Vikrampur, and he exclaimed in Bengali, *Oti valo, oti valo, oti valo ho e!* Very good, very good, very good indeed. This wisest, most educated of men needed nothing more than the most common of expressions to do justice to his deepest emotions.

In the Parisian twilight, from my window on Rue Stephenson, I look out on the Bengali peasants in their fields, the fishermen on their boats, the cattle cart drivers setting out on the road. *Bhawaiya* songs rise from each of their throats, swirling around each other, forming into waves, and gently lapping against my windowsill. "Can you hear them, Fulkumari?" I whisper into the void.

> O beloved *gariyal*
> How long shall I look out at the road for you?
> How shall I tell of my burning grief?
> I've made it a wreath around my neck...

The Return

A Bird with Clipped Legs

The third confinement has ended, and everyone seems determined to go back to normal once and for all. They make a point of parading their freedom under the blazing summer sun, however momentary it may prove to be. But as my life outside the apartment grows vivid again, despondency reigns inside. No matter how hard I try to shake it off, I'm still haunted by Fulkumari's absence. All the spots she once claimed as her own are now filled by an emptiness that overflows into my heart. It's peculiar; the more she's absent in reality, the more my thoughts of her seem to cling to my mind. "I think, therefore I am," Descartes said. "She is, therefore I think" may have been more appropriate.

It has become my ritual to check the letterbox every time I get home, although the only letters I ever receive are official ones, enclosed in white envelopes. They come from social security, the insurance, the bank. Only the name on them is my own. The address below it, however, is as unfamiliar to me as I am to the unthinking machine that printed it out.

Since childhood, this has been my fate—to have my name printed above myriad addresses in cities across the globe. With each address, I plant a tender root, but it isn't long before I have to pull it out once again. The address that may have bloomed in one place is forced to fade away as if it had never been there to begin with. I live in every place as a stranger, so much so that when I pack my bags to leave, it bids me farewell as someone it never knew.

For some misfits, exile is wherever they are—whether in their motherland or not. A person like that has no place in the world. And while we may think we've escaped space, living the ancient dream of migrating like birds, we cannot escape time, the condition that we live in, that surrounds us wherever we go. God may have given us wings, but has clipped our legs in return.

We can fly all we want, but we will never, ever find solid ground to land.

From time to time, in the midst of this meandering existence, an uncanny dawn descends on me. In a state of half-sleep, I find myself unable to recall anything—neither the city where I was born, nor the one where I spent the last night. I'm completely disoriented. But sometimes, just at that juncture, I catch sight of something—outside the window, cloaked in light and darkness, an unknown city gradually rising from its slumber. I begin to see the skyline stretching out across the horizon. And on the outskirts of this city, alongside the maiden sun, a new life is born for me.

I chant the name of this new city under my breath, trying not to let it slip from my memory. Somewhere, an address I've never seen before is seared onto a paper envelope. I memorise every letter, every line of this newborn address. A brand new connection is forged—with the trees, with the wind, with an innocuous blemish on the wall, with a rat. And, with that, once again, the parting begins. The trees, the magic, the mongoose, the rat—all start to leave me for their own destinations.

The Final Return

In the stillness of a night shrouded in shadows, I awake, heart pounding, from a dream steeped in unease. The remnants of my nightmare linger, a cold sweat clings to my skin. As I sit up, the darkness of the room seems to press in around me, a tangible presence. I reach out and flick on the lamp beside my bed. The soft glow banishes the shadows but reveals a sight that steals my breath—a small, motionless form on the wooden floor.

It is Fulkumari!

At that moment, the room feels colder somehow, the walls closer. She has never ventured into my bedroom before, always content with inhabiting the spaces we shared during the day, the corners of the kitchen, the warmth of the living room where our stories were told. And yet, here she is, in the silent sanctuary of my sleep.

I slide from the bed, the floor cold under my feet as I approach her.

"Fulkumari?"

My voice is a whisper, a futile hope that she might stir at the sound of her name. But she remains still, the finality of her departure etched onto her tiny figure. Kneeling, I reach out, my hand trembling as I touch her, half expecting the warmth of life, but finding only the undeniable truth of her silence.

How has she chosen this place, my bedroom, as her last? Perhaps, in her final hours, she no longer sought the solitude of dark corners but the refuge of the bond we used to share. It's a thought both precious and heart-wrenching—that in the end, our desire for closeness and companionship is stronger than everything else.

I sit with her through the night, the silence around us only pressing home the vibrant life she once embodied. Slowly, dawn creeps in, a new day rising on the horizon, its light touching the world with gentle warmth. Yet for me, the morning brings no solace, only the sober task of saying goodbye.

Eternal Recurrence

I bury Fulkumari under the horse chestnut tree, a silent witness to a tiny bond as deep as its own roots in the earth. The streets are still deserted, as if in homage to the days we spent in shared confinement. The Bengali poet Jasimuddin buried his beloved wife under a pomegranate tree, whispering tales of eternal sorrow to his grandson three decades later. I have no grand tales left to tell, watered with tears of sorrow, and no grandchild either to inherit a legacy of grief. Yet the memory of Fulkumari, now part of the earth beneath the tree, clings to me with gentle tendrils.

Like leaves falling quietly, these small sorrows form layer upon layer on our hearts. But perhaps, now, in some silent, unseen way, the chestnut tree will finally answer me. Perhaps, as Fulkumari's essence dances up its roots, its swaying branches and falling leaves will tell me a tale of a time when, in the hour that humanity had to reckon for its recklessness, there remained a corner of the world where a human and a rat could exist in harmony.

We claimed that piece of the world, Fulkumari and I, not by conquest, but by sharing, by recognizing the value in every life, however strange to our own. And now, in this unknown city, under this unnamed tree, below the whispering grass and the timeless dance of nature, our story is taking root. Even as my journey continues, I'll come here to remember, mourn, celebrate, and affirm a silent vow to follow the rhythm of our shared existence, to let it rise and fall with each heartbeat, a melody of love, loss, and eternal recurrence.

Epilogue

Though we know we will never come again, where there is love, life begins over and over again. In my memory, there exist three distinct threads, each shimmering with pure joy and happiness, each lasting no more than a few precious minutes. The third is driving around Dhaka with my wife, putting on one of our favourite CDs, turning up the volume, and watching the outside world blur into a mosaic of colours and sounds.

I came to Dhaka after graduating from medical college, not just to study public health—which I chose to pursue instead of clinical medicine—but also because my fiancée lived there. We'd met and fallen in love during our college years, clasping hands across the chasm of our different religious backgrounds.

Predictably, both our families were strongly opposed to our union. My mother wept, my father threatened disinheritance, and I couldn't fault them for it since I myself had borne witness to the history of war and conflict fueling their reactions. Still, I was encouraged in my love by my political home, the Communist Party, where interreligious marriages were more common and membership was only open to professed atheists.

I never asked my fiancée about the challenges she faced, thinking it better to take care of my own problems and let her handle hers independently. But as a woman, she faced even harsher scrutiny, and her choice to be with a Hindu worked against her all the way down to job interviews. She said I resembled her father—in his honesty, his kind-heartedness, his love for *pat shak*, a salad made from boiled jute leaves that few except the two of us seemed to appreciate.

We were engaged in a battle, she and I, though whether it was against our own insecurities or the world's expectations, I'm not sure. As we pressed on down our path, I found solace in Walt Whitman: *For we are bound where mariner has not yet dared to go. And we will risk the ship, ourselves, and all.*

I disliked Dhaka at first. It seemed to lack a coherent culture, feeling more like a jungle of bricks where the super-rich and the extremely poor led an uneasy coexistence. The city's new elites had come into being in two waves, after the partition of India and the separation from Pakistan. In essence, they were thugs who'd attained their wealth and power by seizing the assets first of Hindus and then of Biharis and Panjabis, falling upon whatever group had been favoured by the country's former rulers only to be abandoned upon their withdrawal from the scene. Even the Dhaka central office of the Communist Party had been seized this way, although my comrades tried to assure me that it was gifted by a supporter of the cause.

Their thuggish origins explain these upstart elites' disdainful attitude. Their only source of pride is their contempt for the less privileged. Everything is a point of mockery to them: status, education, provincial background, accent, attire. If you don't submit to their supremacy, you aren't permitted to climb the social ladder, and if you don't have money, you hardly count as a human being at all. In a residential building, I once saw a sign prohibiting domestic workers from using the elevator. There was no separate elevator for them; they had to use the stairs simply because they were poor.

But then, I discovered Old Dhaka, a small trading hub that the Mughals had established beside the river. As modern Dhaka began to rise right next to it, strangely detached from it rather than organically emerging from it, Old Dhaka retained its narrow streets, its incomplete fort, its rich history. All the original inhabitants of Dhaka still lived here, preserving their own way of life, their dialect, their clothes, their warm, welcoming culture. Somehow surviving next to the monster that had usurped its name, Old Dhaka offered a stark contrast to the modern city's arrogance and superficiality.

The people of Old Dhaka will never let you leave their homes without feeding you first; they have distinct culinary traditions, and their food is extraordinarily tasty. Their festivals are vibrant, and the sense of community they nurture creates a genuine feeling of home, whether for locals or for people passing through. Even Hindus prefer to live in Old Dhaka because they feel safer here. The city reminds me of the provincial towns where I grew up—places free of stark social disparity.

My fiancée moved back in with her family in the new city, while my own journey began on the outskirts of Old Dhaka, at the Intern Doctors' Hostel of Dhaka Medical College. A friend let me stay in his room. It was a small space, shared by six, each with our own dreams and destinies. Two beds, standing like islands three feet apart, were claimed by two of us each. The floor became my bed, shared with another comrade. Four of us weren't even doctors, but merely school friends of my benefactor. Like me, they'd been drawn to the city by the magnetic pull of potential prosperity.

As my fiancée and I settled into our graduate studies, and into our struggle with the judgements surrounding our relationship, the city's dualities shaped our experience and deepened our bond. Dhaka challenged us to find our place and our path amidst its complexity and contradictions, to appreciate its nuanced layers, and to understand how our differences, once a source of division, could become our greatest strength.

After a few years in Dhaka, we felt ready to get married. It would still take some time for our families to accept us, so my comrades organised our wedding. We decided that I would look for work while she continued her studies to pursue a career in medicine. Eventually, after a rather disturbing transition to the private sector, I found a marketing position at a pharmaceutical company—a surprisingly humble choice for a medical doctor at the time. Nevertheless, it provided some stability in our otherwise turbulent life. I got a company car and learned to drive.

Every Friday, the Bangladeshi day of rest, we headed out in the afternoon, driving around aimlessly, our favourite music blasting from the stereo. The car became a cocoon of melodies and memories as we laughed, reminisced, or sometimes just sat in silence. One of our songs, a duet by Tina Arena and Marc Anthony, is with me to this day: *Though we know we will never come again, where there is love, life begins over and over again.* As we approach the Election Commission of Bangladesh, the road gets shaded by giant trees, the sunlight dimly dancing through their leaves. In these brief moments, a sense of joy scuttles up on me, like a playful little pet, nestling in between me and my wife, just as it had with my mother and grandfather during my childhood days in Bogra.

These moments of pure joy, subtle and fleeting as they may be, give us what we need to face whatever may lie ahead. We live the lengths of our lives just for these small moments, as the sunlight dimly dances through the leaves, a familiar, favourite tune fills the air, and we feel the touch of happiness between ourselves and the ones we love.

www.ingramcontent.com/pod-product-compliance
Lightning Source LLC
LaVergne TN
LVHW021316310125
802652LV00016B/49/J